Lonely planet KIDS

LET'S GO
STARGAZING

WRITTEN BY
ANNIE WILLIAMSON

ILLUSTRATED BY
LIZ KAY

CONTENTS

LET'S GO STARGAZING! 8
PACK YOUR KIT 10
WHERE TO START 12

CHAPTER ONE

THE HISTORY OF STARGAZING 15

STORIES IN THE STARS 16
TRAVEL BY THE STARS 17
TELESCOPES THROUGH
THE YEARS 18
ACTIVITY:
NIGHT-SKY SCAVENGER HUNT 20

CHAPTER TWO

STARGAZING AND YOU 23

YOUR VIEWING EQUIPMENT 24
YOUR PLACE ON EARTH 26
USING STAR MAPS 28
TOP TIPS FOR STARGAZING 30
ACTIVITY: STAR HOP! 32

CHAPTER THREE

OUR SOLAR SYSTEM 35

THE SUN 36
THE MOON 38
ECLIPSES 40
MERCURY 42
VENUS 43
EARTH 44
AURORAS 45
MARS 46
JUPITER 47
SATURN 48
URANUS 49
NEPTUNE 50
DWARF PLANETS 51
ASTEROIDS 52
KUIPER BELT 53
COMETS 54
METEORS 55
SATELLITES 56
ACTIVITY: I SPOT 57

CHAPTER FOUR

CONSTELLATION SPOTTER 59

STARS 60
CONSTELLATIONS 62
THE ZODIAC 92
CREATE A CONSTELLATION! 100

CHAPTER FIVE

NIGHT-SKY SPOTTER 103

STAR CLUSTERS 104
NEBULAS 108
GALAXIES 112
ACTIVITY: STAR JOURNEY 116

YOUR STARGAZING DIARY 118
GLOSSARY 120
INDEX 122

LET'S GO STARGAZING!

When the lights dim and night falls, a sky full of stars and other wonders opens up to you. Have you ever wondered exactly what's up there? What is space, and what can you see from your place on Earth? Let's find out!

YOUR PLACE IN SPACE

You live on Earth, which is one of eight **planets** in our Solar System. The planets in our Solar System revolve around the Sun, which is just one of billions of stars in our **galaxy**. And our galaxy, the Milky Way, is just one of billions of galaxies in the universe! In this book, we will look at planets, stars, galaxies and more as you discover your place in space.

STELLAR FACT

On a clear night, you can usually see hundreds or even thousands of stars in the sky.

SEASONS CHANGE

The more you study the sky, the more you'll discover. Through the seasons, what you can spot in the night sky shifts and changes. Can you find any patterns?

LET THIS BOOK BE YOUR GUIDE

In this book, you'll find everything you need to know to be an expert stargazer. You'll discover the different objects in the night sky and learn about patterns in the stars and the stories associated with them. In the second half of the book are spotter guides to help you learn the names of the objects you might spot and know what to look for when. There are also lots of stargazing tips and fun activities for you to try!

READY TO REACH FOR THE STARS? LET'S GO... STARGAZING!

PACK YOUR KIT

The first thing you'll need for a stargazing session is a clear night. The second is a kit containing handy items to help you on your journey of discovery across the night sky. Pack your bag so you can be ready at any time!

RED-LIGHT TORCH

Your eyes need about 20–30 minutes to adjust to the darkness (see p.24). A red-light torch helps you light up things that you need to see in the dark, such as your notebook or field guide, without dazzling your carefully adjusted eyes.

MOBILE PHONE

Take a phone with you in case you need to get in touch with anyone. You can also use apps or websites to find out what you can spot and when. Use a red-screen option if possible to avoid spoiling your night vision.

PORTABLE CHARGER

Make sure you have a way of recharging your phone if the battery runs flat.

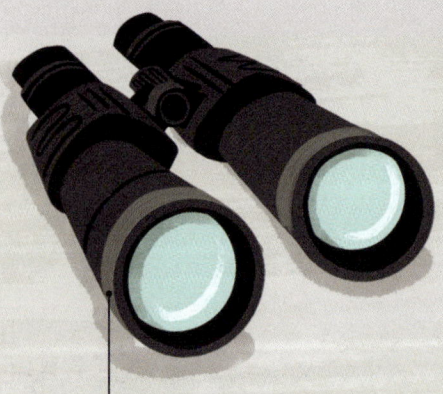

BINOCULARS AND/OR TELESCOPE

You can see a lot with just your eyes, but if you want to discover even more phenomena in the night sky, you might want to borrow or invest in binoculars and/or a telescope. There's more on these on pages 24–25.

NOTEBOOK AND PEN

Bring a notebook and pen to take notes on your sightings: what you see, the date and time. See pages 118–119 of this field guide for an example of how to set up a stargazing diary.

BACKPACK
Put it all together in a sturdy backpack!

STELLAR TIP
Always take an adult with you when you go out at night. Stargazing is more fun with company!

BLANKET
Don't hurt your neck! Lie down on a blanket so you can comfortably gaze up at the sky. Alternatively, ask a grown-up to pack a reclining chair.

WARM CLOTHES
Even on warm days, the evenings and nights can get cool. Bring layers, such as a jumper, coat and woolly hat, so you can wrap up warm no matter the weather.

DRINKS AND SNACKS
Prepare to be outside for a while, and be sure to pack plenty of drinks and snacks.

COMPASS
Bring a compass with you or use the compass app on a phone. This will help you read star maps and find your way around the sky.

FIELD GUIDE
Take this book with you when you venture out into the night. The spotter sections on pages 58–115 will help you identify what you see.

11

WHERE TO START

As you begin your stargazing journey, keep these super-stellar tips in mind.

FIND A CLEAR VIEW

Check the weather before you plan an evening of stargazing. A clear, dark night is best! Ask your grown-up to drive to a safe and public countryside location to see the night sky at its best.

Choose a night just right for stargazing!

The Milky Way above Tenaya Lake, California, USA

CHANGE WITH THE TIMES

As Earth moves through space, our view of the night sky changes. Check night spotter apps and websites to find out which **celestial** objects or special events might be visible from your area at any time.

KNOW YOUR POSITION

North or south, east or west – your position on Earth affects what you see in the sky. Look carefully at pages 26–29 to understand your place on the planet and how to use the correct star charts for you.

STELLAR TIP

Every night is different! Get out regularly to look for patterns and see how the sky changes in your area.

USE YOUR GUIDE

Read through this guide before you venture outside. It will help you to understand what is happening in the sky, which in turn helps you know what to look for and how to recognise what you see. You should also take it with you when you go stargazing, to help you identify your sightings.

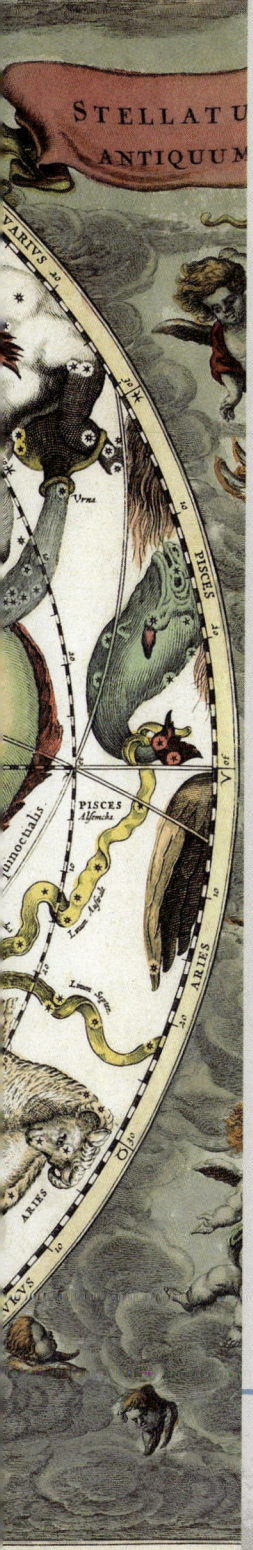

CHAPTER ONE

THE HISTORY OF STARGAZING

Thousands of years ago, early stargazers created pictures from the shining dots in the sky and spun stories about what they saw. These stories were passed down through generations and have become ingrained in many cultures. These early stargazers also carefully mapped the night sky, taking measurements and noting seasonal changes that helped them to navigate the world. In more recent times, technological developments, such as the invention of the telescope, have allowed people to study the sky in great detail. Nowadays, **astronomers** use technology to see further into space than ever before.

LET'S GO!

STORIES IN THE STARS

For thousands of years, humans have tracked patterns in the night sky. Very early stargazers didn't have the instruments to explore or understand the science of space and would often look at the skies through a mystical eye.

The Egyptian god Ra had the body of a man and the head of a falcon, and was often depicted with a solar disc above his head.

GODS IN THE SKY

Many cultures looked to the skies to explain their world. For example, in the Middle East of 3,000 years ago, the Babylonian people searched the sky for signs from the gods. They thought that changes in weather or unusual events, such as solar eclipses or shooting stars, could be warnings of famine or war. Other cultures thought the stars and other celestial objects were the gods themselves, or souls in the sky. In ancient Egypt, the Sun was thought to be the great god Ra, creator of all other gods and humans.

LEGENDS ABOVE

The ancient Greeks made up stories to explain the patterns of people, animals and objects they picked out in the stars. Usually, these myths were related to legends and gods. Many other cultures did the same thing, so stories vary across the world. For example, what's known as the Plough in the UK (see p.64) is called the Big Dipper in the US because of its resemblance to a ladle shape. The Macedonians of southeast Europe see the same pattern as a group of thieves, while the Inuit of northern Canada tell stories of a caribou in the sky.

STAR STORIES

Discover some ancient stories of different star patterns on pages 58-115.

TRAVEL BY THE STARS

When humans began to see repeating patterns in the sky over months and years, they started to use the night sky for more than just stories. They discovered that they could find their way by the stars and tell the time of year too.

Artists created illustrations to show patterns in the night sky. This 1883 painting depicts the pattern of stars above South Africa.

MEGA MAP

Imagine being out at sea, with no landmarks around you to find your way. Then look up – way up – to the sky above. Suddenly, the entire night sky becomes a mega map to guide you! For sailors in the Northern **Hemisphere**, for example, the Pole Star (see p.64) could show them which way was north, helping them to find their bearings. Familiar **constellations** at certain times of the year became landmarks for these travellers.

STELLAR FACT

Stonehenge – a fascinating circle of stones built in England around 5,500 years ago – was carefully designed to align with the movements of the Sun. During the summer solstice (the longest day of the year), the Sun rises perfectly over one of the main stones.

COSMIC CALENDAR

As early astronomers began to track the stars, they recognised that they appeared to shift and show different constellations at different times of the year. Once people plotted these patterns on star maps, they began to use the stars to plan for the changing seasons. They could even predict occurrences such as blood-red moons and solar **eclipses** (see pages 40–41).

TELESCOPES THROUGH THE YEARS

Since ancient times, people have been striving to get a closer look at the stars. In the early 1600s, an invention came along that finally allowed them to do so: the telescope!

1608

Hans Lippershey, a spectacle maker in the Netherlands, created the very first telescope. His device featured a pair of lenses that made things that are far away appear closer than they are.

It is believed that Lippershey invented the telescope after seeing children playing with two lenses in his shop.

1609

Italian scientist Galileo Galilei turned the early telescope up towards the sky. He built his own telescope that could magnify objects to appear even closer. Among other things, he discovered four moons orbiting Jupiter. This discovery helped support the idea that the Solar System revolved around the Sun and not Earth, as people first thought.

1781

British-German astronomer William Herschel used a 12 m- (40 ft-) long telescope to spot the planet Uranus for the first time.

Herschel's Telescope

1668

English scientist Isaac Newton replaced the lenses with a pair of mirrors, making an even bigger and more powerful telescope.

1933

The first **radio waves** were detected from outer space. Since then, telescopes have been invented that detect radio emissions from stars and galaxies, rather than light.

Leviathan Telescope

1845

On his estate in Ireland, English astronomer William Parsons built a huge telescope, nicknamed the 'Leviathan'. For over 70 years, it was the largest telescope in the world.

Mauna Kea Observatory

1964

The Mauna Kea Observatory was founded in Hawaii, USA. Instead of being bigger than what came before, the telescopes that were built here were higher! Sitting at the top of a dormant volcano, above the clouds, they have some of the clearest views of the night sky.

Hubble Space Telescope

1990

The Hubble Space Telescope launched into **orbit**. It looks deep into space from within space itself!

2021

The largest telescope yet was launched into space. Instead of orbiting Earth like the Hubble Space Telescope, the James Webb Space Telescope orbits the Sun.

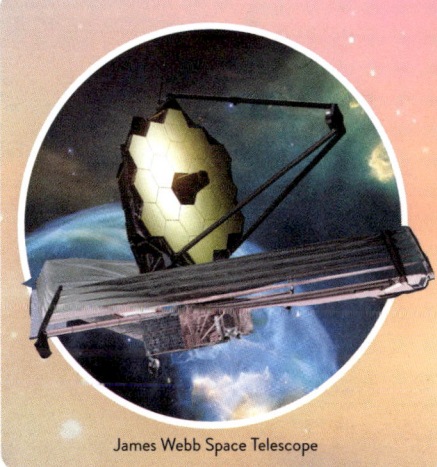
James Webb Space Telescope

NOW

You can use telescopes to get a spectacular zoomed-in view from your very own back garden. See pages 24–25 to find out more about the options available to stargazers like you.

ACTIVITY: NIGHT-SKY SCAVENGER HUNT

Start your stargazing journey with this **cosmic** activity. Wait for a clear night, then see if you can spot any of the items in this stellar scavenger hunt.

STELLAR TIP
Check online or use a stargazing app to discover the best time to see **meteor showers** and spot **comets**.

The Moon
(see pages 38–39)

A planet
(see pages 42–50)

A **shooting star**
(see p.55)

A **satellite**
(see p.56)

A constellation
(see pages 62–99)

A **nebula**
(see pages 108–111)

The Milky Way
(see pages 112–114)

Andromeda Galaxy
(see p.114)

MONTHLY CHALLENGE

It might be difficult to spot everything in one night. Instead, you could set yourself a Stargazer Challenge for a month. Draw a grid that's seven squares across by four squares down and make a note of what you see each night. Can you spot all the items in the list over the course of four weeks? Try tracking the phases of the Moon, too, to see its monthly sequence. Look at pages 38-39 to help you.

MAY 1ST	MAY 2ND	MAY 3RD	MAY 4TH	MAY 5TH	MAY 6TH	MAY 7TH
Waning gibbous Ursa Minor, Ursa Major, Draco Venus	Half-moon Ursa Minor Mars	Waning crescent Couldn't see much else, it was quite cloudy	Waning crescent Two satellites	Waning crescent		
MAY 8TH	MAY 9TH	MAY 10TH	MAY 11TH	MAY 12TH	MAY 13TH	MAY 14TH

MESSIER CATALOGUE

In the 18th century, astronomer Charles Messier began a catalogue of deep-sky objects that could be observed from the Northern Hemisphere. All the objects on the list can be seen using simple telescopes, so spotting them has become a popular challenge for **amateur** spotters. The catalogue includes 110 items in total, including incredible sights such as M1 (the Crab Nebula), M51 (the Whirlpool Galaxy) and M45 (the Pleiades).

STELLAR FACT
The 'M' in the names of the objects stands for Messier.

Crab Nebula (M1)

Whirlpool Galaxy (M51)

The Hubble Space Telescope has provided scientists with incredible images of 87 of the 110 objects in Charles Messier's catalogue.

CHAPTER TWO

STARGAZING AND YOU

As you begin your stargazing journey, get to know the equipment and the maps that will guide you. Learn about your place on Earth to help you discover the cosmic wonders that might appear above your eyes. Read star maps, use stargazing apps and even use your hands to measure space! There's an entire universe out there waiting to be revealed once you learn how.

LET'S GO!

YOUR VIEWING EQUIPMENT

A great deal of equipment is available to help hobbyist astronomers like you see the stars – from small binoculars to giant telescopes! Consider what might suit you best.

STELLAR TIP

Remember to use a red-light torch if you need to see anything else in the dark (such as this guide or your snacks) so you don't undo your eyes' adaptation to the dark.

THE UNAIDED EYE

With your eyes alone, you may be able to spot countless stars, impressive constellations and up to five shining planets. To get the best view, let your eyes adjust to the darkness before you stargaze. Be patient and start with 20–30 minutes outside at night to let your eyes adapt. This is called **dark adaptation**. The pupils (black holes) in the centre of your eyes will gradually get bigger and allow more light in.

BINOCULARS

Binoculars use two side-by-side telescopes to magnify the night sky, allowing you to see amazing detail, such as craters on the Moon and faraway galaxies. They come in different sizes and are described with two numbers, such as 12 x 50 ('twelve by fifty'). The first number is how many times the binoculars magnify an object (so a pair of 12 x 50 binoculars magnifies an object twelve times). The second number is the diameter of the larger pair of lenses in millimetres. The bigger the lenses, the more light they collect, and the more you can see.

Binoculars are a good start for amateur astronomers.

TELESCOPES

Telescopes will give you the closest view of the night sky. If you're serious about stargazing, you might like to invest in your own telescope. You could also see if there are any available to borrow from local astronomy groups.

STELLAR TIP

Choose a telescope that's a convenient size for you to use. If it's too big, you're unlikely to get it out very often!

There are many different types of telescopes, so it's important to choose the right one for you.

Many astronomical telescopes reverse the image that you see. Because of the way the mirrors reflect the light into your eye, the image you receive is inverted and upside down. It might take a little getting used to, but this is perfectly normal!

DIFFERENT TYPES

Refracting telescopes, like this one, use curved lenses, while reflecting telescopes use curved mirrors. These are the two most common types of telescopes.

Some telescopes have a camera attachment to capture photos of whatever can be seen through the lens.

Digital telescopes can use smart technology to help find and track stars.

STELLAR TIP

Telescopes take practice and patience. Using this book to find your way around the night sky will help you know where to point any equipment!

All telescopes require a mount to keep them steady. A mount can also help you point your telescope in different directions.

YOUR PLACE ON EARTH

Our spherical planet spins as it orbits the Sun and travels through space. What you can see in the night sky will depend on your position on Earth. So, let's get to know your place on the planet!

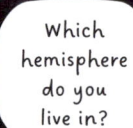

Which hemisphere do you live in?

HEMISPHERES

An imaginary line runs horizontally around the middle of our planet. This is called the **Equator**. The half of the planet above the Equator is called the Northern Hemisphere. The half below the Equator is called the Southern Hemisphere. Your view of the sky is different depending on which hemisphere you are in.

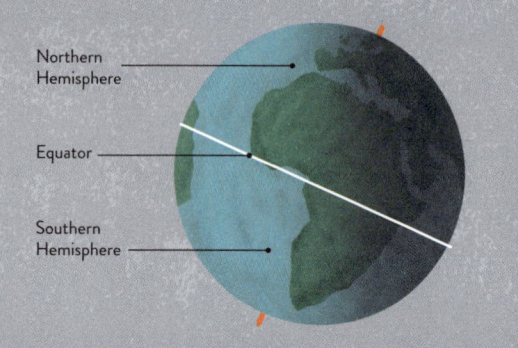

CELESTIAL SPHERE

Astronomers imagine that Earth is inside a giant ball where the stars and planets live. This is called the **celestial sphere**. Just like Earth, the celestial sphere has an equator around the middle. And just as Earth has a North Pole and a South Pole, the celestial sphere has the North Celestial Pole and the South Celestial Pole. These poles and the stars near them appear to stay in place as everything else rotates.

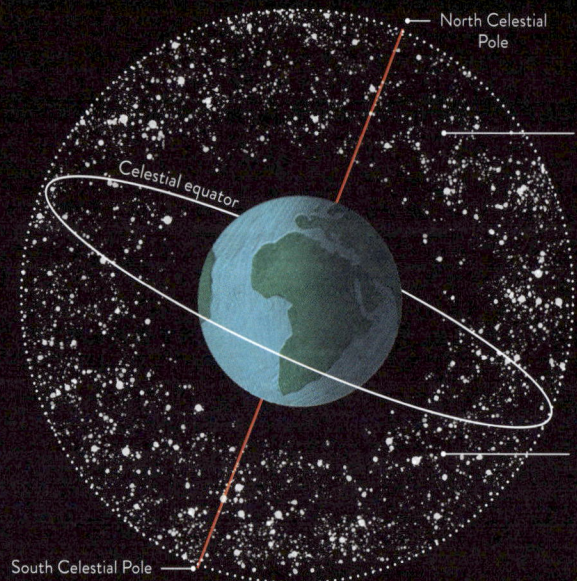

If you live in the Northern Hemisphere, you will mostly see celestial objects that exist in the north half of the celestial sphere.

If you live in the Southern Hemisphere, you will mostly see celestial objects that exist in the south half of the celestial sphere.

SEASONS

An imaginary line runs down through the centre of Earth, from the North Pole to the South Pole. This is called Earth's axis, and it is slightly tilted. Earth rotates around this axis as it makes its trips around the Sun. One full rotation is one full day – 24 hours. A full trip around the Sun is a year. The seasons are caused by the tilt. When Earth is tilted towards the Sun, it's summer in the Northern Hemisphere and winter in the Southern Hemisphere. When it's tilted away, the seasons are reversed.

STELLAR TIP

Some constellations are visible all year round, while others can only be seen at certain times of the year. Some are visible from both hemispheres – others are visible from just one or the other. Consult a stargazing website or app to understand what is visible to you and when.

DEGREES

Astronomers measure the distance between stars in degrees. You can use your hands to roughly calculate these distances yourself. Standing with an arm outstretched, the width of your little finger is roughly equal to 1 degree; three middle fingers held together is about 5 degrees; a closed fist is approximately 10 degrees, and so on (in the order shown in the illustrations).

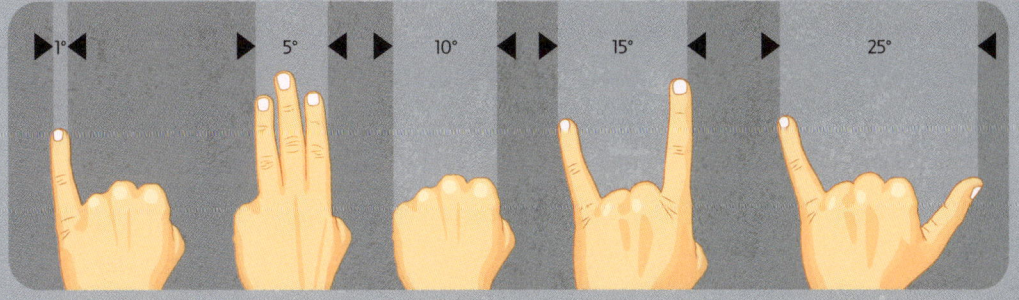

USING STAR MAPS

Because our planet is always moving, what you see in the night sky is constantly changing. A single map cannot cover it! Star maps show the portion of the night sky that you can see from a specific location, at a certain time.

READING THE STARS

Maps of the stars are different from maps of places on Earth. For a start, they are usually round! The outer edge of the circle represents the **horizon** (at ground level), and the centre point shows what you would see if you were at the North Pole or South Pole and looked straight up. East and west will look the wrong way around when you look at a star map flat, but hold it up to the sky over your head and they'll be in the right place!

These star maps show the major constellations in the Northern Hemisphere (left) and Southern Hemisphere (right). You will see different parts of the map in the sky depending on the time of year.

NORTHERN HEMISPHERE

STELLAR TIP

Brighter objects in the night sky are shown on star maps with bigger dots or symbols than others. Try looking for these in the sky!

MANY MAPS

There are different maps for the Northern and Southern Hemispheres, and maps for the different seasons of the year too. You can even find maps for different times of day! Some maps are available as **planispheres**, with a cut-out window. If you line up the date with the time, you can spin the map to show only what is visible in that specific night sky. You can buy simple planispheres, as well as a variety of star maps, in shops or online. There are also digital star maps available online or through various stargazing apps.

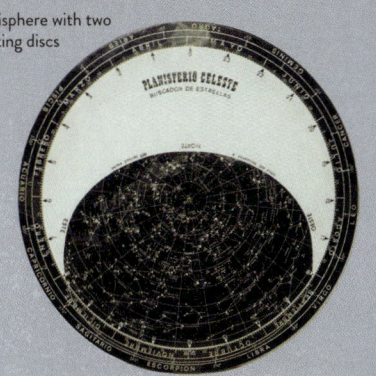

Planisphere with two rotating discs

SOUTHERN HEMISPHERE

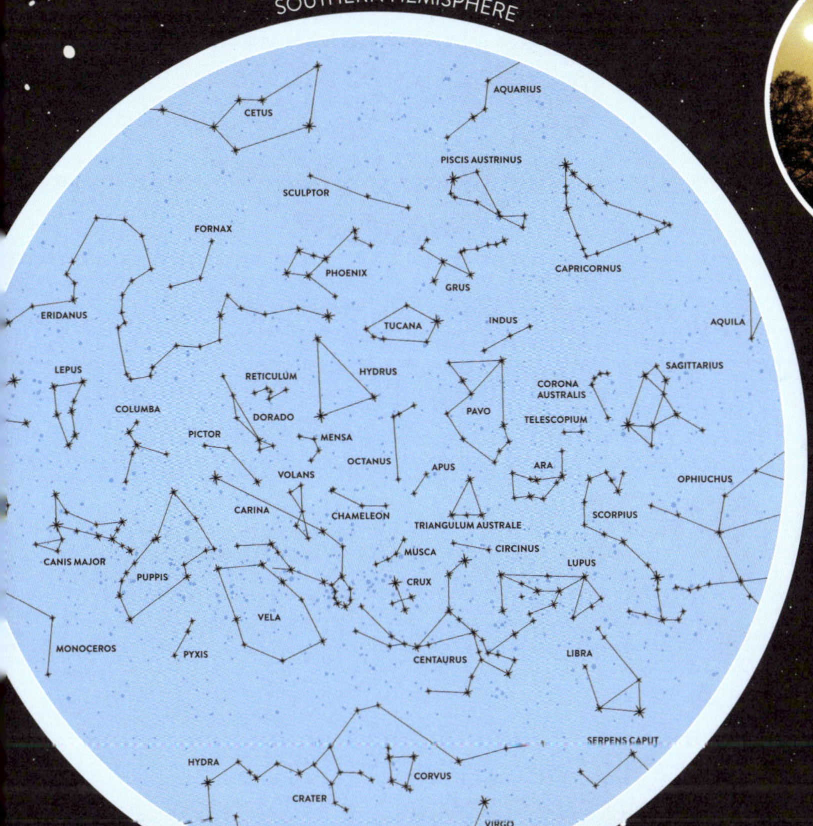

The **ecliptic** is the path the Sun appears to take through the sky. The Moon and planets seem to follow this path too. If you can see the ecliptic on star maps, it can help you to spot the planets in the night sky.

TRY IT YOURSELF

Can you make your own star maps? Draw the stars and constellations you see in the sky during each season of the year. Don't forget to mark the date and time so you can refer to your maps again.

TOP TIPS FOR STARGAZING

You know your place on Earth and you've got your kit packed. You've chosen your equipment and have your maps at the ready. It's time to stargaze! Try these top tips to get the most out of your stargazing experience.

FIND LOW LIGHT

City lights can outshine the stars. This is called **light pollution**. If you're stargazing from your own backyard, turn off the lights inside the house to keep your viewing area as dark as possible.

Los Angeles, USA

BUDDY UP

Always stargaze with at least one other person. Never go out into nature on your own. Take an adult with you and share your sightings with each other. You might even discover local astronomy clubs that you could join to stargaze in a group.

KNOW YOUR LIMITS

You will never spot everything in one night. Consult your constellation and night sky spotter guides carefully to see which celestial objects might be visible on the night you choose.

LOOK AWAY

Sometimes the best sights will appear when you're not looking directly at them. Try looking just next to the object you're hoping to see, and it might appear out of the corner of your eye. This is called **averted vision**.

BE PATIENT!

Stargazing requires a lot of patience. First, you need to wait 20–30 minutes to let your eyes adjust to the darkness. Avoid using a bright light or screen in that time. Then you might need to wait longer again to spot a shooting star or satellite. You may also find it difficult to make out the various constellations or distinguish planets from stars when you first start. Keep practising, and you'll soon become a true expert of the great night sky.

STAY SAFE

Follow these final tips for a safe and smooth stargazing experience.

 DO plan ahead. Keep your stargazing kit ready (see pages 10–11). Check the weather before you go. A clear night is best, and never go out in storms.

 DON'T stargaze on private property (only stargaze in public places or at your own house).

 DO leave nature as you found it. Never litter, and take everything back home with you.

 DO enjoy the experience! The more you relax, the more hidden wonders will show themselves to you.

ACTIVITY: STAR HOP!

A wonderful way to get started on your stargazing experience is to star hop: finding the most recognisable patterns in the sky and using them to 'hop' to other sights. Try these star hopper challenges to locate some of the brightest stars in the sky.

NORTHERN HEMISPHERE

CHALLENGE 1: LOCATE POLARIS

Best time to see: Year-round

First, find the Plough **asterism** in the Ursa Major constellation (see p.64). The two stars on the right are called the pointer stars. Draw an imaginary line from the bottom star to the top star, then carry on. This will lead you to Polaris (also called the Pole Star or North Star), which is part of the constellation Ursa Minor. Polaris sits above the North Pole, so locating it also shows you which way is north.

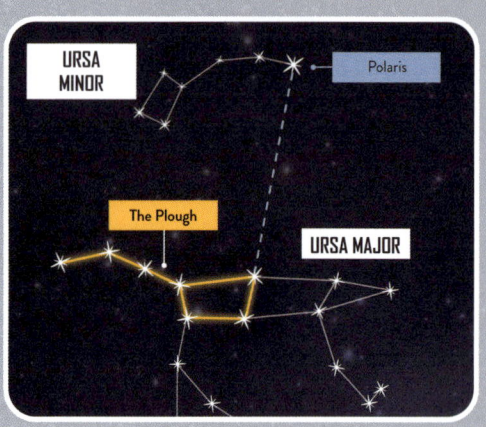

CHALLENGE 2: LOCATE ALDEBARAN

Best time to see: December to February

Aldebaran is a bright orange star in the Taurus constellation (see p.94). To find it, first look for Orion's Belt, a line of three stars in the constellation Orion (see p.77). Follow the line of the belt out through Orion's shield and it will lead you to Aldebaran, which is part of the Hyades **open cluster** of stars (see p.94).

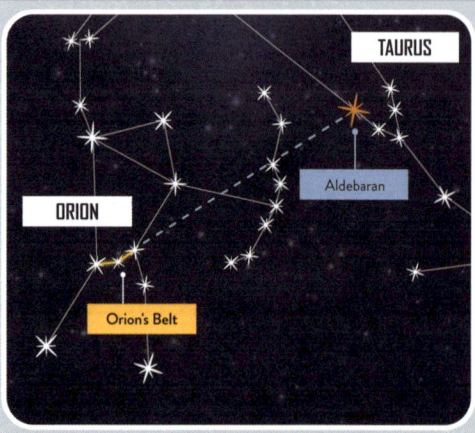

SOUTHERN HEMISPHERE

CHALLENGE 1:
LOCATE THE SOUTH CELESTIAL POLE

Best time to see: Year-round

First, find the constellation Crux (see p.65). It is a cross shape made of four stars. Draw an imaginary line from Gacrux at the head of the cross to Acrux at the foot. Continue this line approximately another four times the distance between Gacrux and Acrux, and you will arrive at the South Celestial Pole. Unlike the North Celestial Pole, there is no star to mark its location.

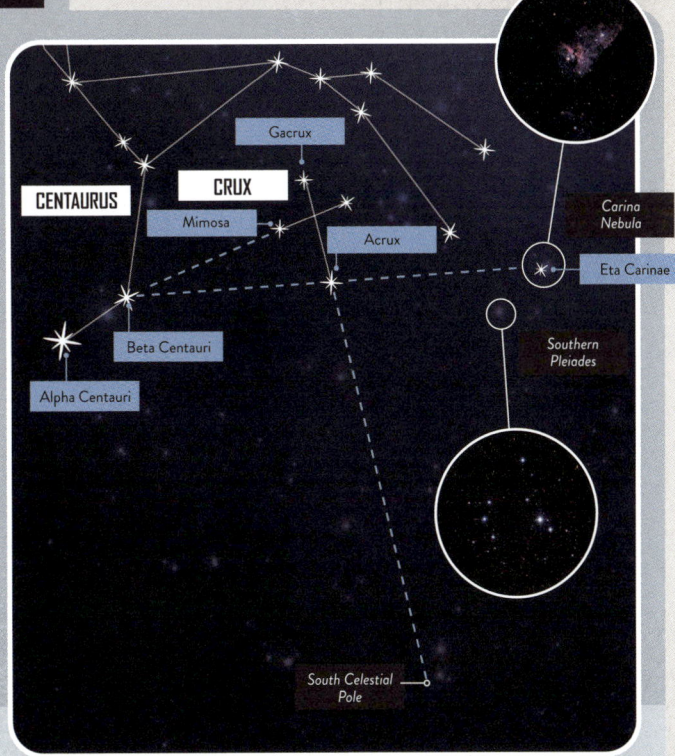

CHALLENGE 2:
LOCATE ALPHA CENTAURI AND BETA CENTAURI

Best time to see: March to September

Back at Crux, follow the crossbar outwards from the star Mimosa, and you will reach Alpha Centauri and Beta Centauri (see p.85) in the Centaurus constellation. Alpha Centauri is the third-brightest star in the sky. Its neighbour Beta Centauri is slightly dimmer.

CHALLENGE 3:
LOCATE ETA CARINAE AND THE SOUTHERN PLEIADES

Best time to see: February to July

From Beta Centauri, draw an imaginary line passing through Acrux and out the other side. Here you will find the Carina Nebula. Near its centre is the Eta Carinae star. Not far from this is a fuzzy patch called the Southern Pleiades (see p.106). You can see this with the **unaided eye**, but use your binoculars for an even more impressive view.

CHAPTER THREE

OUR SOLAR SYSTEM

Our Solar System is everything within the gravitational pull of the Sun. This includes eight planets and their moons, smaller dwarf planets, comets, **asteroids** and meteoroids. Many of these celestial objects can be seen with the unaided eye, and even more wonders will reveal themselves to you through binoculars and telescopes. What can you spot?

LET'S GO!

THE SUN

The Sun is the key piece that holds the Solar System together. It is so large that its **gravity** pulls all objects in the Solar System towards it – from planets and asteroids to space debris – causing them to swing around and around the Sun in orbit.

WARNING!

Although the Sun is the biggest and brightest object in our Solar System, you should never look at it directly. In fact, it is SO bright that it can damage your eyes.

ANOTHER STAR

The Sun is actually a type of star. It looks so much bigger than the other stars in the sky because it is much closer to us. Although it could contain a million Earths, it is considered medium-sized.

SUN

EARTH

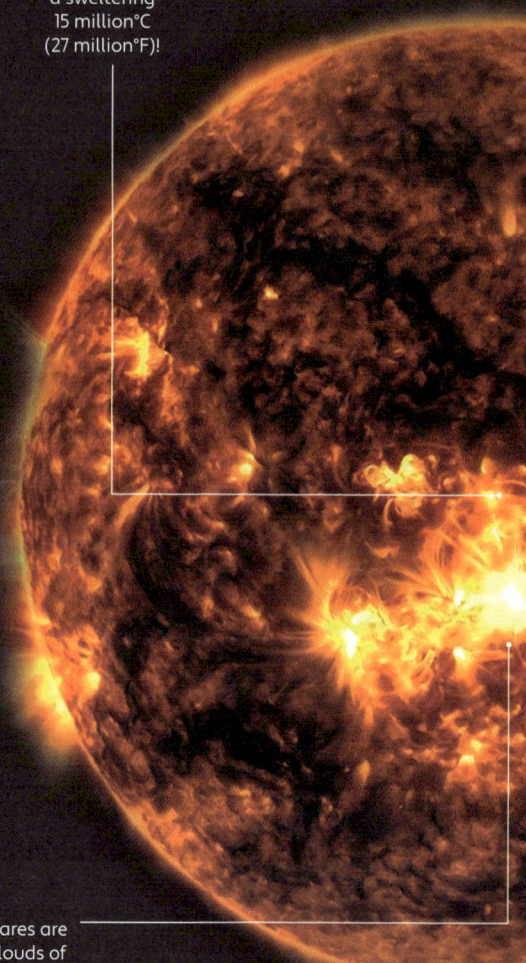

The core of the Sun is a sweltering 15 million°C (27 million°F)!

Solar flares are huge clouds of hot gas that burst out of the surface.

SUN POWER

Like all other stars, the Sun is a giant ball of super-hot gas – mainly hydrogen and helium. At the core, nuclear reactions fuse hydrogen atoms to form helium. In the process, a huge amount of energy is released. It travels out from the core in the form of heat and light.

The corona is a wispy layer of hot gas that surrounds the Sun.

STAR WORDS

The Latin word for Sun is 'sol'. Many Sun-related terms contain this word, such as 'solar power'. Others contain the word 'helios'. In ancient Greek mythology, Helios was the god of the Sun. He travelled across the sky from east to west each day in a chariot. For example, 'heliosphere' is the area of space surrounding the Sun that is affected by solar wind (charged particles that flow out of the Sun).

STELLAR FACT

Curiously, the corona is even hotter than the Sun's surface. It reaches temperatures as high as 2 million°C (3.5 million°F).

The surface of the Sun is about 5,500°C (10,000°F).

STARGAZER CHALLENGE

Although you should never look directly at the Sun, you can look at the beautiful sky it creates. Sunrise will appear to your east. Sunset will appear to the west. Note down the time you see these on the first day of every month. Do you notice how the times change? Because of the tilt of our planet, daylight lasts longer in the summer and days feel shorter in the winter.

You can see some amazing colour combinations in the sky at dawn and dusk.

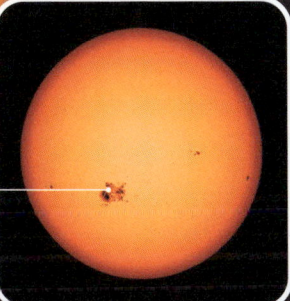

Darker spots on the Sun are cooler areas called sunspots.

37

THE MOON

The Moon is one of the best night-sky objects to observe as you begin your stargazing journey. You can see it with your bare eyes but can view even more detail through binoculars or a telescope. If you observe it over the course of a month, you'll notice a pattern too!

MOONLIGHT

The Moon is the second-brightest object in the sky, after the Sun. However, it doesn't emit any of its own light. Instead, we can see it because it reflects light from the Sun. From our position on Earth, we only ever see one side of the Moon. This is because of the way the Moon orbits Earth. The other side is referred to as the 'far side'. You'd need to travel into space to see it!

STARGAZER CHALLENGE

Try the activity on pages 20–21 to track the phases of the Moon over the course of a month. Can you see how it changes?

PHASES OF THE MOON

As the Moon orbits our planet and Earth orbits the Sun, the shape of the Moon in the sky appears to change. These changes are known as the phases of the Moon. Over 29.5 days, the Moon goes through a full cycle of phases – then starts all over again!

Waxing Gibbous

First Quarter (Half-Moon)

Waxing Crescent

New Moon

LIGHT AND DARK

The largest dark areas on the Moon are called seas. Long ago, astronomers thought they were full of water, but these 'seas' are really areas where molten lava once flowed, leaving behind large plains of dark rock. Lighter areas on the Moon are mountainous regions.

COUNTING CRATERS

The Moon is covered in dusty rock. When asteroids or comets crash into the surface, they leave large holes known as craters. Look through your binoculars to see if you can spot these.

STELLAR FACT

'Waxing' means getting bigger, and 'waning' means getting smaller. 'Gibbous' comes from on old word meaning 'hump'. A gibbous moon is bigger than a half-moon but smaller than a full moon.

Full Moon

Waning Gibbous

Third Quarter (Half-Moon)

Waning Crescent

39

ECLIPSES

An eclipse only happens every once in a while, when the Sun, Moon and Earth line up in space. During an eclipse, a celestial object that would normally be visible is hidden from view, either partially or completely.

WARNING!

Even during an eclipse, you should never look directly at the Sun without special equipment.

Use special eclipse glasses to watch an eclipse safely.

TOTAL SOLAR ECLIPSE

During a total solar eclipse, the Sun seems to disappear in the sky, and the day goes dark for a short time. This happens when the Moon and Sun appear to be the same size in the sky and the Moon passes directly in front of the Sun, covering it completely. On Earth, this casts a shadow that moves as the Moon travels. Anyone in the shadow is plunged into darkness for a few minutes.

The Sun's corona (see p.37) is visible around the edge of the Moon during a total eclipse.

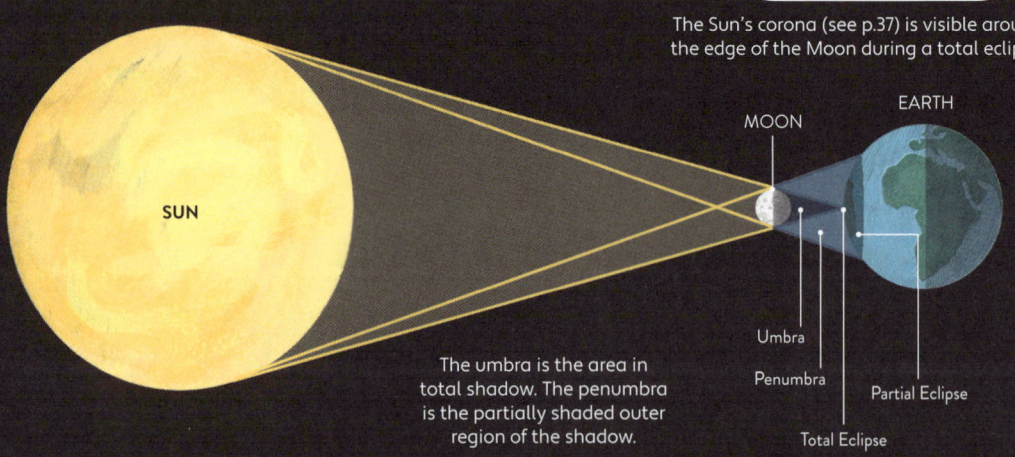

The umbra is the area in total shadow. The penumbra is the partially shaded outer region of the shadow.

ANNULAR AND PARTIAL SOLAR ECLIPSE

The Sun is actually 400 times larger than the Moon, but it is also 400 times further away. When the Moon is at its furthest distance from Earth, it looks smaller in the sky. If it passes in front of the Sun at this point, it won't entirely cover it. Instead, we see a smaller dark circle in front of the Sun, called an annular eclipse. During a partial eclipse, the Sun, Moon and Earth aren't perfectly aligned, so people on Earth see only part of the Sun covered up. People outside the area covered by the Moon's shadow in a total or annular eclipse will see a partial solar eclipse.

TOTAL LUNAR ECLIPSE

A total lunar eclipse occurs when the Moon disappears behind Earth (relative to the Sun) and passes through Earth's shadow. The whole Moon is covered and often appears to glow an orange or red colour from the limited sunlight that reaches it. This is called a 'Blood Moon'. Lunar eclipses are safe to look at directly – and spectacular to see!

Note: Images are not to scale.

MOON STORY

Imagine seeing the Moon change to a deep blood red, with no explanation why. Long ago, people didn't have the science to understand what was happening, so they explained the strange phenomenon by creating their own stories. For example, the Inca in South America believed that a jaguar was attacking the Moon and the Moon was bleeding. To ensure the jaguar did not then come to Earth, they shook spears, shouted and howled at the Moon to scare the creature away.

A Blood Moon

STELLAR TIP

The Moon also has partial and penumbral eclipses. Check astronomy websites and apps to learn when these will happen in your area.

41

MERCURY

Mercury is the smallest planet in the Solar System, and the planet closest to the Sun. Because of these two facts, it is quite tricky to see!

> **THE STATS**
>
> **Name:** Mercury
> **Meaning:** the Roman messenger god with speedy winged feet
> **Visible:** best from near the Equator
> **Best time to see:** shortly before sunrise or shortly after sunset, depending on the time of year

MORE ABOUT MERCURY

Mercury is a rocky planet, like Earth. Its surface is covered in craters and cliffs. It moves quickly around the Sun, making a full loop in just 88 days.

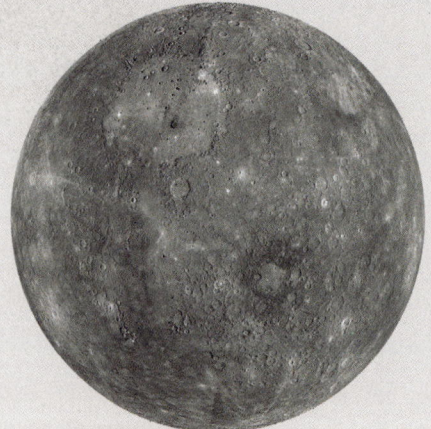

Mercury

HOW TO SPOT

As is the case with all planets, Mercury makes no light of its own. We can see it because it reflects light from the Sun. However, it stays close to the Sun, which makes it hard for us to see due to the bright glare. The best time to spot it is shortly before sunrise or shortly after sunset. Look close to the horizon and see if you can pick out this tiny light grey dot in the sky.

STELLAR TIP

Stars appear to twinkle in the sky because their light passes through and distorts in Earth's **atmosphere**. Because planets are much closer to us, the sunlight reflected off them is stronger and not distorted in the same way. When you're looking for planets, look for dots of light that do not twinkle!

EQUIPMENT TIP

When it is visible, you should be able to see Mercury with the unaided eye. But you would need a very big telescope to make out any individual features on the surface because the planet is so small.

VENUS

Venus is a wonderful object to spot. At its brightest, it is the third-brightest object in the sky after the Sun and the Moon.

> **THE STATS**
>
> **Name:** Venus
> **Meaning:** the Roman goddess of beauty and love
> **Visible:** Northern and Southern Hemispheres
> **Best time to see:** two hours before dawn and two hours after sunset

UNFRIENDLY TWIN

Venus is another rocky planet and is a similar size to Earth. It is sometimes called 'Earth's evil twin' because it is much less hospitable than our life-filled planet. Venus's atmosphere is full of carbon dioxide, and clouds of smelly sulphuric acid surround it. Beneath the clouds, a super-hot surface bubbles amongst volcanoes and towering mountains.

EQUIPMENT TIP

Venus is so bright that it can easily be spotted with the unaided eye. And there's no point using a large telescope to try to see the surface – it is covered in clouds! However, with a small telescope or binoculars, you can see that Venus has different phases, just like the Moon.

HOW TO SPOT

Look for the brightest object in the sky that isn't the Sun or the Moon! Venus appears as a brilliant white light, so bright that sometimes it is even visible in the daytime. Depending on the time of year, the best time to see it is two hours before sunrise or two hours after sunset. Later than that, and it will likely have followed the Sun out of sight. Check your stargazing website or app to find out when it is likely to be in the sky near you.

STELLAR FACT

Because Venus appears at dawn at some points of the year, and other times at dusk, the ancient Greeks thought it was two separate stars. It wasn't until the mid-4th century BCE that they discovered it was the same object.

EARTH

You don't need a telescope to see your own planet! But let's learn a little more about how it compares to other objects in space.

THE STATS

Name: Earth
Meaning: the ground

AT THE CORE

Earth is one of the four rocky inner planets of the Solar System. It has an outer crust covered in oceans, mountains and the land you live on. Below that are the upper and lower mantles, made of super-hot solid and molten rock. At the centre of Earth is its core: a huge metal ball with temperatures up to 6,000°C (10,000°F).

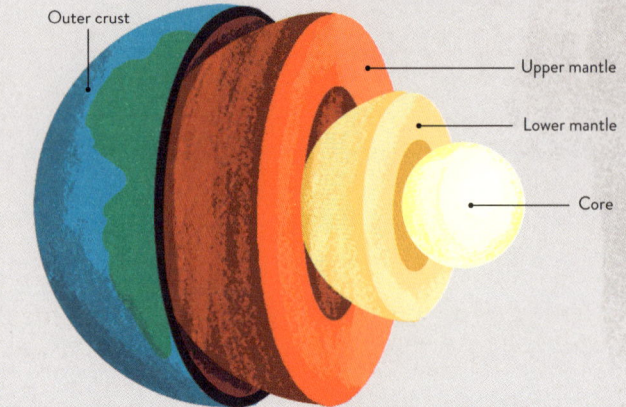

Outer crust
Upper mantle
Lower mantle
Core

JUST RIGHT

Scientists say that Earth exists in the Goldilocks Zone – not too far from and not too close to the Sun, and just right for life! Earth is the only planet in the Solar System known to have liquid water on its surface. This allows it to support plants, animals and you!

VIEW FROM SPACE

If you were looking at Earth from space, as astronauts do, you would see a blue ball with green and brown patches and swirling white clouds.

AURORAS

One of the most incredible sights for sky-gazers to catch is the northern or southern lights, officially known as aurora borealis and aurora australis.

THE STATS

Name: aurora borealis (northern lights) and aurora australis (southern lights)
Meaning: the Roman goddess of dawn
Visible: mostly close to the North and South Poles
Best time to see: check stargazing websites and apps

If you use a long exposure setting on a camera and look at the photo or screen, the colours will appear even more vivid!

DANCING LIGHT

Auroras look like shimmering sheets, rays, beams or arcs of coloured light in the night sky. They are caused when solar storms on the Sun emit electrically charged particles that travel towards Earth. When these particles mix with Earth's atmosphere, the oxygen and nitrogen in our air glow green, pink and purple. We see this as the northern lights (aurora borealis) in skies near the North Pole and the southern lights (aurora australis) near the South Pole.

HOW TO SPOT

Auroras are a special occurrence and do not happen all the time. They are normally seen close to Earth's poles, but they can sometimes be spotted further away when solar storms are particularly strong. Check a website or app to find out where you can see them and when. As with all stargazing, let your eyes adjust to the darkness and be patient as you wait for this light show to appear.

MARS

Mars is often called the 'red planet' because of its rust-coloured surface. Luckily, this colouring gives a helpful hint for spotting it in the night sky!

> **THE STATS**
>
> **Name:** Mars
> **Meaning:** the Roman god of war
> **Visible:** Northern and Southern Hemispheres
> **Best time to see:** check stargazing websites and apps

Human-made robots roam the surface of Mars to learn more about it.

RUST AND MOONS

Mars is the last of the four rocky planets in the Solar System. Iron oxide (rust) on the surface gives it its reddish appearance. Mars has two moons that orbit the planet: Phobos and Deimos. They are too small to spot though.

HOW TO SPOT

Mars is another bright object in the sky. Look for a non-twinkling light with a reddish or orange colour, along the ecliptic (see p.29). However, be aware: Mars moves around the sky and is less visible at certain times. It is best to spot it when it is close to Earth and at its brightest. As it travels around the opposite side of the Sun, it is much further away and harder to see.

STARGAZER CHALLENGE

Use a telescope to look at the surface of Mars. Can you spot icy white patches at the poles?

The icy patches will appear bright compared to the rocky red surface.

JUPITER

Jupiter is the biggest planet in the Solar System, and another bright object shining in the sky.

GIANT JUPITER

Jupiter is mostly made of hydrogen and helium (like the Sun) and so is known as a 'gas giant'. It is more than twice as massive as all the other planets in the Solar System combined. The gases swirl around and sometimes act like liquid because of the great pressure, but there is no solid surface on this planet. With a powerful telescope, you can see stripes and spirals of cloud.

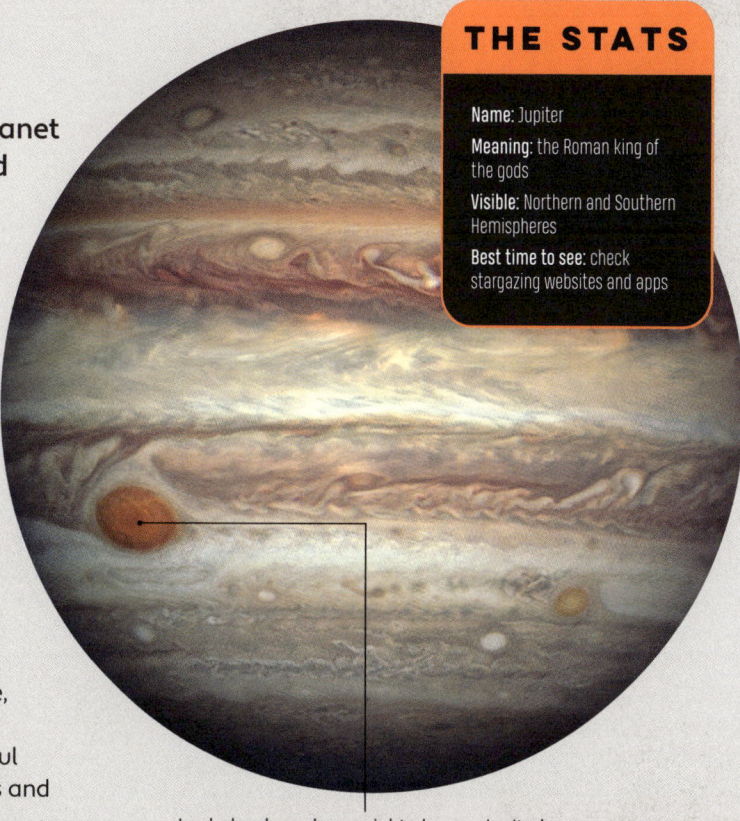

Look closely and you might also see Jupiter's Great Red Spot, a storm that has been raging on the planet for at least 150 years.

THE STATS

Name: Jupiter
Meaning: the Roman king of the gods
Visible: Northern and Southern Hemispheres
Best time to see: check stargazing websites and apps

MOON SPOTTING

So far, 95 moons have been spotted orbiting Jupiter. If you look through binoculars or a telescope, you may be able to spot some (or even all) of the four largest moons. They are called Ganymede, Io, Callisto and Europa.

Jupiter and its four largest moons

HOW TO SPOT

Jupiter reflects the Sun's light, just like the other planets, and its clouds reflect it strongly! This makes Jupiter brighter than stars in the sky. Look along the ecliptic (see p.29) on a clear night for a bright off-white object that appears much bigger than the stars around it. Check websites or apps to discover when it will be most visible to you.

47

SATURN

The last of the planets that you can see easily with the unaided eye, Saturn has a surprise waiting for you if you use powerful binoculars or a telescope: vast, spectacular rings!

THE STATS

Name: Saturn
Meaning: the Roman god of agriculture and wealth
Visible: Northern and Southern Hemispheres
Best time to see: check stargazing websites and apps

SUPER SATURN

Saturn is the second-largest planet in the Solar System and is another gas giant. Like Jupiter, it is made mostly of hydrogen and helium. Bands of clouds swirl around due to winds stronger than a hurricane on Earth. Saturn has at least 274 known moons – more than any other planet.

Saturn's rings are twice as wide as the planet.

STELLAR TIP

Although they are wide, Saturn's rings are very thin. It's quite likely that you'll only see the three largest rings, and sometimes none at all!

STANDOUT SIGHT

Other planets have rings, but Saturn's are the most impressive. There are seven rings surrounding the planet, each made of orbiting pieces of ice, rock and dust. These can be as small as a pebble or as big as a mountain.

HOW TO SPOT

Saturn takes 29 years to orbit the Sun, so it appears to stay in the same area for years at a time. Once you know where it is, you should be able to find it again. Look for a bright, yellowish object along the ecliptic (see p.29), about the same brightness as the brightest stars but without their twinkle.

URANUS

Uranus is so far away from Earth that it is extremely hard to see with the unaided eye. It is the seventh planet from the Sun and the first of the two ice giants.

> **THE STATS**
>
> **Name:** Uranus
> **Meaning:** the Greek god of the sky
> **Visible:** Northern and Southern Hemispheres
> **Best time to see:** check stargazing websites and apps

ICE GIANT

Uranus is a cold, windy place. It is the third-largest planet and is known as an ice giant. Most of the planet is made of an icy mix of water, methane and ammonia, with a swirling, slushy surface. Methane gas in the atmosphere makes the planet look bluish-green.

Unlike all the other planets, Uranus spins on its side.

RINGS AND MOONS

Uranus has two sets of faint rings and 28 known moons. You need a powerful telescope to search for these.

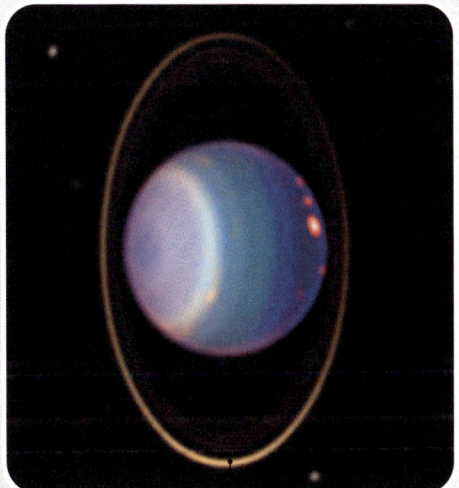

Because Uranus spins on its side, its rings are upright.

HOW TO SPOT

You'll need binoculars or a telescope to spot Uranus clearly. Consult a website or app to learn where to look and when. With your binoculars, you should see its bluish-green colour. With a telescope, you might be able to make out a disc shape too.

NEPTUNE

The last of the eight planets in our Solar System, Neptune is impossible to see with the unaided eye. But if you use a telescope or binoculars, you'll discover this blue wonder.

THE STATS

Name: Neptune
Meaning: the Roman god of the sea
Visible: Northern and Southern Hemispheres
Best time to see: check stargazing websites and apps

ICE TWINS

Like Uranus, Neptune is a cold, windy ice giant. Winds whip across the surface at speeds up to 2,000 kph (1,200 mph) – nine times stronger than any storm on Earth. Icy water, methane and ammonia swirl above a dense rocky core. Methane gas in the atmosphere makes the planet appear blue. Neptune has five rings and 16 known moons.

HOW TO SPOT

Consult a website or app to learn where to look and when, then get out your binoculars or use a telescope to spot this distant planet. With binoculars, you should see something that looks like a star. With a powerful telescope, you might be able to make out a disc shape and the planet's bluish tinge.

STARGAZER CHALLENGE

Using a powerful telescope, can you spot Neptune's largest moon, Triton?

STELLAR FACT

Neptune is so far away from the Sun that even at midday on Neptune, the light would be as dim as twilight on Earth.

DWARF PLANETS

As well as the eight planets of the Solar System, there are five dwarf planets: smaller planets that do not have a gravity strong enough to be called a planet in their own right.

STARGAZER CHALLENGE

Can you spot the heart shape on Pluto's surface in this photo, captured by the New Horizons spacecraft?

FAMOUS FIVE

Discovered in 1930, Pluto was once considered the ninth planet in our Solar System. When two similarly sized objects were discovered, astronomers decided that there should be a new category of smaller 'dwarf' planets, and Pluto was moved down to this category in 2006. A number of dwarf planets have now been recognised, including Makemake, Eris, Ceres and Haumea. Scientists believe there may be many more of these smaller planets still to be discovered!

HOW TO SPOT

Pluto is so far away that it is difficult for amateur astronomers to spot. The best view is from space itself. In 2015, a NASA spacecraft called New Horizons flew past Pluto and sent photos back to Earth. Thanks to these, we now know that Pluto has mountains and valleys, craters and glaciers.

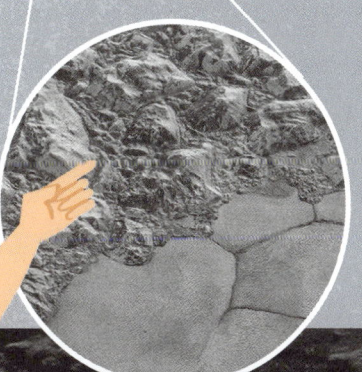

This photo taken from New Horizons shows an area of Pluto 80 km (50 miles) wide.

ASTEROIDS

Between Mars and Jupiter lie millions of rocky objects orbiting in a ring called the Asteroid Belt.

STELLAR FACT
If you put all the asteroids in the asteroid belt together, they would be less massive than Earth's Moon.

Jupiter · Asteroid Belt · Earth · Venus · Sun · Mercury

ROCKY LEFTOVERS

Asteroids are relatively close to Earth but are so small they can be tricky to spot. The biggest and brightest asteroid is Vesta, which can sometimes be seen with the naked eye. For others, you'll need binoculars or a telescope and a very clear night. Asteroids are spread far apart in the asteroid belt – on average, about 1,000,000 km (620,000 miles) separate each one!

HOW TO SPOT

When you think you've spotted an asteroid, look at the same spot in the sky a few hours or nights later. Has the object moved in relation to the stars around it? If so, it's likely an asteroid! If it has stayed in the same place, it is probably a star.

KUIPER BELT

A donut-shaped ring of ice and rocky debris circles the Solar System beyond Neptune. This faraway region is called the Kuiper Belt.

THE STATS

Name: Kuiper Belt
Meaning: named after astronomer Gerard Kuiper (1905–1973), who proposed the existence of this region in 1951
Visible: not to unaided eyes

ICY HOME

The Kuiper Belt is home to millions of icy objects as well as four of the five dwarf planets, including Pluto. Many comets (see p.54) come from here.

STELLAR FACT

Ceres is the only dwarf planet not located in the Kuiper Belt. It is found in the Asteroid Belt, between Mars and Jupiter.

EXPLORING THE KUIPER BELT

The Hubble Space Telescope orbits Earth above the atmosphere, where it can take much clearer pictures than we can get from the ground. It has made many discoveries within the Kuiper Belt, including moons around Pluto. The New Horizons spacecraft was the first to travel past Pluto (see p.51) and continues to explore the Kuiper Belt today.

MYSTERIOUS BEYOND

Beyond the Kuiper Belt, surrounding the entire Solar System like a sort of bubble, is the Oort Cloud. Scientists have never seen this mysterious area, but believe it could contain trillions of icy pieces of space debris and is where many of the comets that visit the inner Solar System originate.

Note: Image is not to scale.

COMETS

Unlike stars, planets and asteroids, comets appear in the night sky for a short time, then disappear again, out into the far reaches of the Solar System. They can be an impressive sight to spot!

FROZEN LEFTOVERS

Like asteroids (see p.52), comets are left over from the creation of the Solar System 4.6 billion years ago. These frozen chunks are made of ice, dust and pieces of rock. They can be as big as a small town! They come from the Kuiper Belt and Oort Cloud (see p.53).

HOT AND COLD

Comets have an unusual orbit, travelling quite close to the Sun and then swinging way out towards the Kuiper Belt or Oort Cloud. This means that when they are far away, they are very cold, but when they travel close to the Sun, they heat up. As they do, the ice turns to gas, and the comet trails tails of gas and dust. This is what we can see from Earth.

HOW TO SPOT

Consult a website or app to find out when comets are due in the skies near you. Some pass regularly while others won't return for hundreds or thousands of years. Even through a telescope, most comets appear only as a faint smudge that moves over hours or days. If you do spot a comet without using a telescope, you might see its short, misty tail. Brighter comets appear around once every three or four years. These sometimes develop longer glowing tails that are easier to catch sight of.

STELLAR FACT

Halley's Comet is a famous comet because it helped astronomers to realise that comets return and must therefore orbit the Sun. When a bright light was spotted three times, decades apart, Edmond Halley predicted that it was in fact the same comet and would return. He was right!

Halley's Comet appears in the night sky every 75–76 years.

THE STATS

Name: Halley's Comet
Meaning: named after English astronomer Edmond Halley
Visible: Northern and Southern Hemispheres
Best time to see: the year 2061!

METEORS

Another amazing phenomenon every astronomer hopes to see is a shooting star – which is not actually a star at all! In fact, it is a small rock burning up as it passes through the atmosphere.

A ROCK OF MANY NAMES

A meteoroid is a rock in space. This includes grains of dust and small asteroids. When a meteoroid enters Earth's atmosphere, it is called a meteor. These meteors normally burn up in the atmosphere and light up the sky as quick streaks of light known as shooting stars. If the meteor makes it all the way to Earth's surface, it is called a meteorite.

A meteorite often has little pits on its surface.

METEOR SHOWERS

Although you can't predict individual shooting stars, there are certain times of the year when they are more likely. When many meteors occur at once, it is called a meteor shower. These happen when Earth passes through the debris of a comet or broken bits of an asteroid on its journey around the Sun, so they take place at the same time each year. Consult stargazing websites and apps to discover when you can see them for yourself.

STELLAR FACT

Meteor showers are named after the constellation they appear to come from when you see them in the sky.

STELLAR TIP

Look for shooting stars when the Moon isn't bright, so it doesn't outshine them.

HOW TO SPOT

Don't look directly at the namesake constellation. Instead, look at nearby constellations and see if you can spot any shooting stars. Choose a clear night and a place away from bright lights, then get comfy! Lie back and watch the sky with patience.

SATELLITES

A trail of Starlink satellites

The celestial objects that we've looked at so far are natural – they exist naturally in space. But there are also loads of other objects out there that humans have created, including artificial satellites.

WHAT IS A SATELLITE?

A satellite is any object that orbits another. Natural satellites include moons, which orbit planets. Even Earth is a satellite, orbiting the Sun! Humans send artificial satellites into space for many different reasons. Some satellites beam communications signals (such as GPS signals) down to Earth. Others track weather and climate changes. Starlink satellites provide Internet coverage for the world and can appear as a moving chain of lights across the night sky for a day or two after they've been launched.

There are thousands of Starlink satellites in space. Most are launched in chains of between 20 and 30.

HOW TO SPOT

Many satellites use solar panels for energy. They reflect the Sun, making it possible for you to spot them on a clear night. Look for satellites just before sunrise or after sunset. The biggest clue to know whether your sighting is a satellite is to watch if it moves steadily across the sky.

INTERNATIONAL SPACE STATION

The International Space Station (ISS) is the biggest human-made object in the sky. Astronauts stay on this orbiting laboratory about 400 km (250 miles) above us for months at a time to carry out research in space. The ISS orbits Earth, so you can see it pass overhead. It can appear as bright as Venus or Jupiter and might have a yellow tinge. It moves across the sky for a few minutes before it disappears again. Check a website or app to find out when it might be in the sky near you.

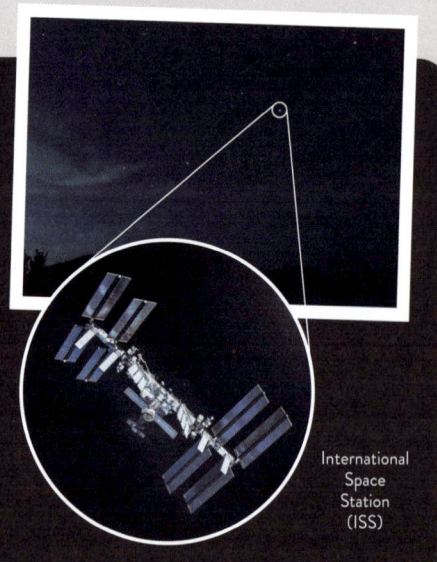

International Space Station (ISS)

ACTIVITY: I SPOT...

Follow these steps to help identify whether you are looking at a star, a planet, a meteor or a satellite.

STEP 1
Choose an area of sky to observe. Lean back and watch patiently. When you spot an object you'd like to identify, move on to step 2.

STEP 2
Follow this chart to identify your find.

STEP 3
Write down what you spot in your logbook. Don't forget to note where you saw it and when.

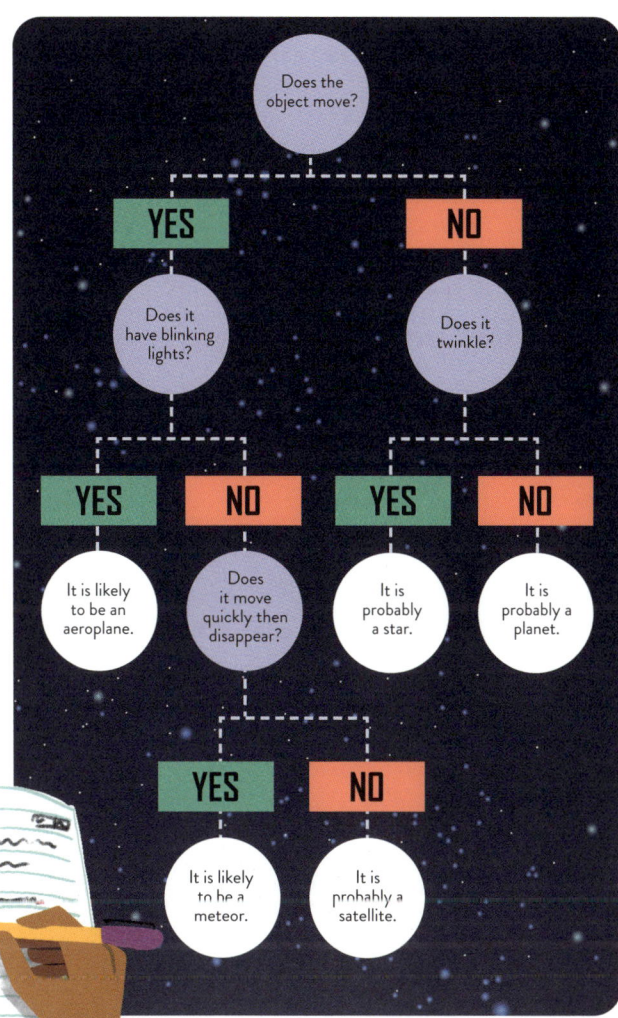

CHAPTER FOUR

CONSTELLATION SPOTTER

In this chapter, you'll discover constellations to seek out on your stargazing journey. Read the following pages to learn more about each one, then see which constellations you can spot in the night sky depending on where you are and when you're looking. Pay close attention to the hints, tips and tricks to help you.

A box of stats tells you the official name of the constellation and where this name comes from. Check here to find out where on Earth the constellation can be seen from, and when it is best to look.

Diagrams show what the constellations look like in the night sky.

Once you've found the constellation, see if you can complete these extra challenges.

Many constellations are named based on stories people told a long time ago. Some of these stories are found here.

STARS

Before we look at constellations, we need to look closer at the sparkly dots that make up these patterns in the sky: the stars! These giant balls of hot gas vary throughout their lives and have life cycles just like us, only theirs last millions of years or more.

HEAT AND LIGHT

Deep inside a star, intense heat and pressure cause hydrogen atoms to fuse together, creating helium atoms. This process releases both heat and light, forming a huge ball of gas that we see as a star.

LIFE CYCLE OF A STAR

AVERAGE STAR

Stars then shine for millions or even billions of years as main sequence stars, or average stars. This is the longest stage of their life. Our Sun is an average star.

STELLAR NEBULA

Stars are born inside swirling clouds of gas and dust called nebulas (see p.108). You can see these cloudy patches across the night sky.

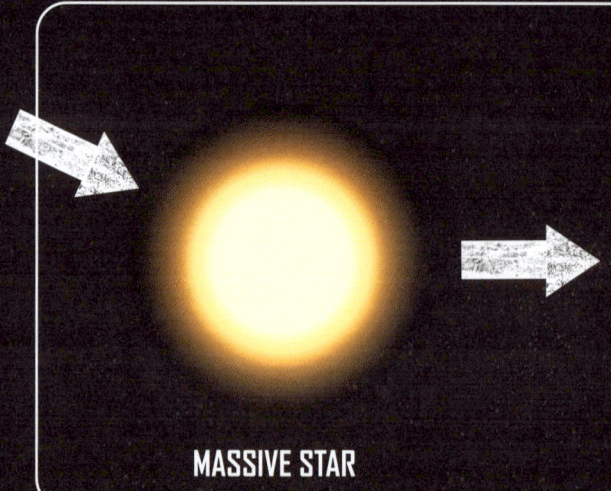

MASSIVE STAR

RED GIANT
Near the end of their lives, as they run out of fuel, average stars begin to swell into red giants. The star cools and its light becomes reddish-orange rather than bright yellow.

PLANETARY NEBULA
When red giants die, they create a new nebula. The star shrinks, spreading gas and dust out into space and creating a cloud that can look like a glowing planet. A small white dwarf star remains in the centre until it stops shining completely.

WHITE DWARF

STARGAZER CHALLENGE
Using binoculars or a telescope, can you spot any red giants in the night sky? Remember to look for stars that appear red.

SUPERNOVA
Bigger than an average star, a massive star swells into a red supergiant. As it burns out, it explodes as a supernova, bursting matter far out into space. This matter can collect into new stellar nebulas, where new stars will be born! Some supernovas collapse in on themselves and form a **black hole** (see p.98), while others create a neutron star – a tiny object with a super-strong gravitational pull.

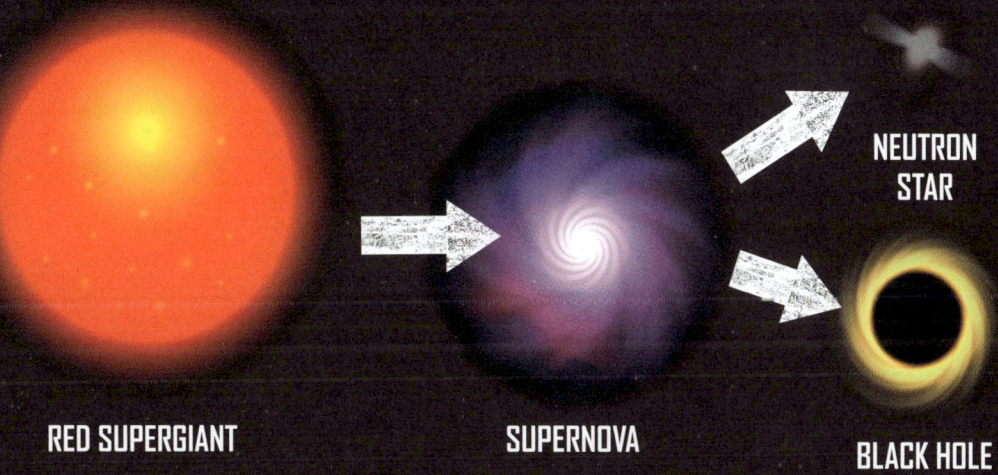

RED SUPERGIANT — SUPERNOVA — NEUTRON STAR / BLACK HOLE

CONSTELLATIONS

Constellations are patterns of stars in the sky. Some constellations are vast, while others include only a few stars, but all of them are visible with the unaided eye.

Northern Hemisphere constellation map

DOT-TO-DOT

Constellations are like dot-to-dot pictures in the sky. Thousands of years ago, people spotted patterns in the stars and connected the dots to make shapes such as animals and objects. There are now 88 recognised constellations. Some of these clearly look like the shapes they represent, while others only look slightly like them, or not at all!

MIDNIGHT MARKERS

Constellations have become important tools for mapping the night sky. They can be used as markers for directions, or as pointers to direct the eye to another stellar wonder.

STELLAR FACT

The largest constellation is Hydra (see p.82). Its shape is made up of 17 stars and spans over 100 degrees (see p.27) of the night sky – more than any other constellation.

The constellation Hydra

ASTERISMS

An asterism is a smaller pattern of stars that is not one of the official 88 constellations. Sometimes an asterism is a portion of a larger constellation, such as the Plough within Ursa Major (see p.64). Other asterisms include stars from a number of different constellations. The Winter Triangle (see p.78), for example, is formed of bright stars from three different constellations.

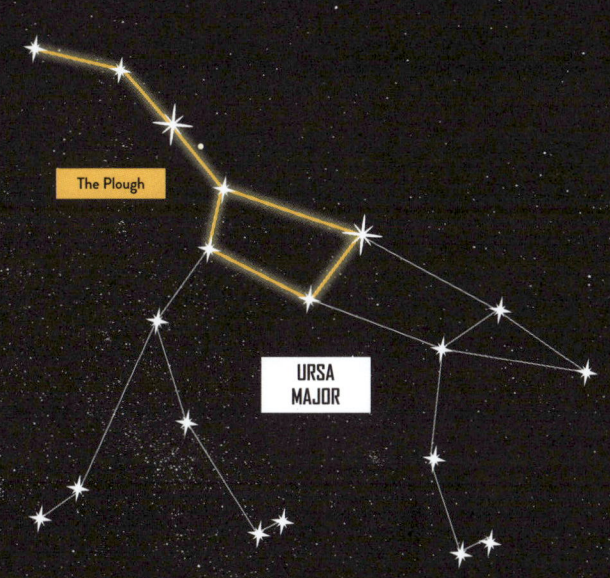

THE NAME GAME

Many constellations still have the names given to them by ancient Greek astronomers. Others were named by sailors hundreds of years ago. Within the constellations, each star has a name of its own. Often these are related to the constellation itself. The brightest star is named 'alpha' after the first letter of the Greek alphabet. The second-brightest star is 'beta' after the second letter of the Greek alphabet, the third is 'gamma' and so on. For example, the brightest star in the Tucana constellation (see p.84) is called Alpha Tucanae.

URSA MAJOR AND URSA MINOR

These bears are two of the most well-known constellations in the Northern Hemisphere. They contain many wonderful things to spot on your stargazing journey.

THE STATS

Constellation: Ursa Major
Represents: a great bear
Visible: Northern Hemisphere and northerly parts of the Southern Hemisphere
Best seen: most of the year but best viewed March to April

URSA MAJOR

Ursa Major, or the 'Great Bear', is the largest constellation in the Northern Hemisphere. Within it you'll find a famous asterism (see p.63) called the Plough.

The Great Bear

THE PLOUGH

The Plough looks like a big saucepan or ladle and is often called the Big Dipper. If you draw an imaginary line between the two stars on the far right of the Plough and keep on going up, you will reach Polaris, also known as the Pole Star or North Star (see p.32).

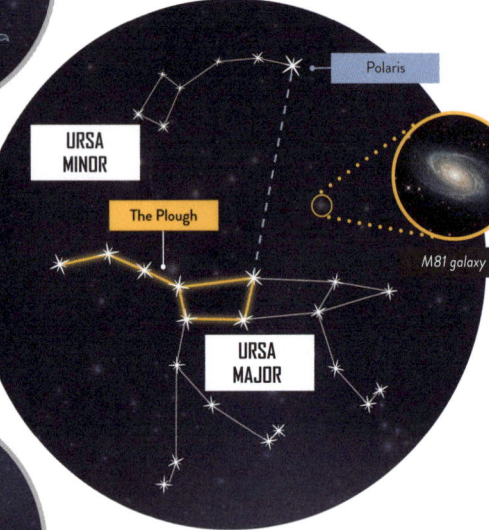

URSA MINOR

Once you've found Polaris, you'll see Ursa Minor, or the 'Little Bear'. This constellation is also known as the Little Dipper because it looks like the Plough (Big Dipper).

THE STATS

Constellation: Ursa Minor
Represents: a little bear
Visible: Northern Hemisphere and northerly parts of the Southern Hemisphere
Best seen: all year round

STARGAZER CHALLENGE

Using binoculars, can you spot the M81 galaxy just above the Great Bear's back?

STAR STORY

In Greek mythology, Ursa Major was a wood nymph called Callisto, and Ursa Minor was her son, Arcas. The god Zeus took a liking to Callisto. In a fit of jealousy, his wife Hera turned Callisto into a bear. Later, Zeus turned Arcas into a bear too and placed mother and son amongst the stars as Ursa Major and Minor so they could be together forever more.

CRUX

Crux is the smallest of all 88 constellations in the sky. Made up of only four stars, it is also called the Southern Cross.

THE STATS

Constellation: Crux
Represents: a cross
Visible: Southern Hemisphere and southerly parts of the Northern Hemisphere
Best seen: most of the year but best viewed April to September

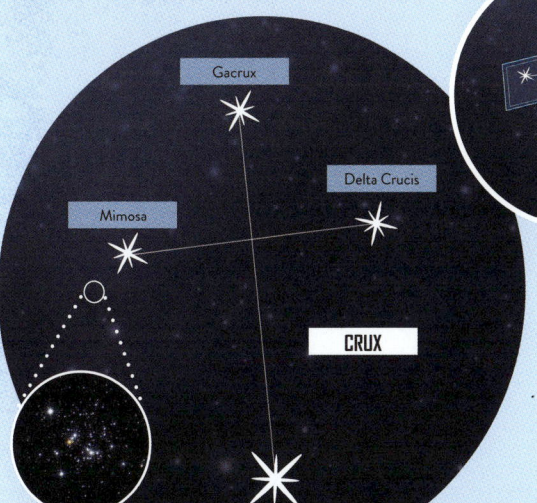

Southern Cross

STARGAZER CHALLENGE

Using a telescope, look for the bright and colourful Jewel Box Cluster (see p.107). It is near a star named Mimosa in the cross.

GUIDING THE WAY

Like Polaris and Ursa Minor in the Northern Hemisphere, Crux can be used in the Southern Hemisphere to guide the way. If you follow the line from Gacrux to Acrux and then go four and a half times further, you'll find the South Celestial Pole.

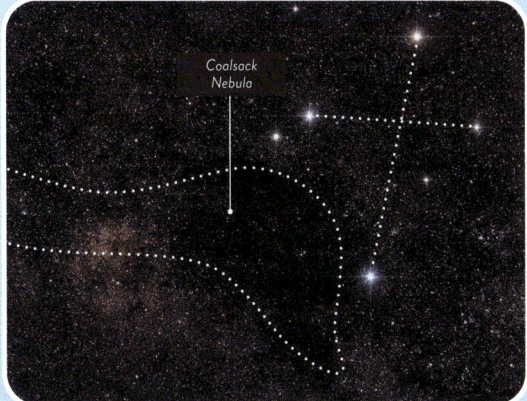

CLOUDY SKIES

Darkening the sky in one corner of Crux is the Coalsack Nebula. This thick cloudy patch of dust blocks our view of loads of stars in the Milky Way. In Australian Aboriginal culture, this nebula is said to form an emu's head in the sky.

STELLAR FACT

This constellation is so well known that it appears on not one, not two, but five countries' flags: Australia, New Zealand, Brazil, Samoa and Papua New Guinea.

The flag of New Zealand

SOUTHERN HEMISPHERE

DRACO

Draco the dragon soars in the sky above the North Pole, so this constellation can be seen in northern skies all year round. You might also be able to catch it from northern parts of the Southern Hemisphere.

THE STATS

Constellation: Draco
Represents: a dragon
Visible: Northern Hemisphere and northerly parts of the Southern Hemisphere
Best seen: May to June

SOARING DRAGON

Draco's tail sits between Ursa Major and Ursa Minor (see p.64). From there, the dragon swoops out towards Hercules (see p.73). This constellation is made of 15 stars, including bright stars Thuban and Eltanin.

STARGAZER CHALLENGE

Use a telescope to look near the dragon's neck. Can you spot a fuzzy bright patch? This is called the Cat's Eye Nebula.

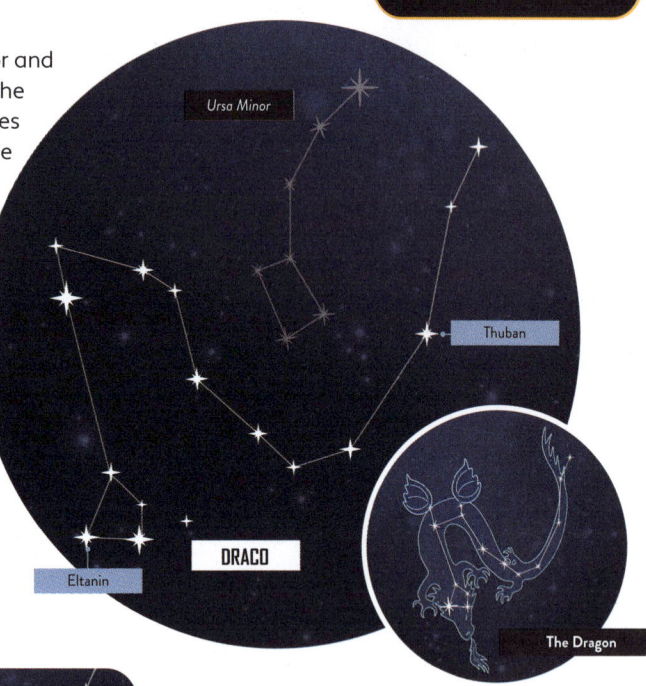

STAR STORY

In Greek mythology, this constellation represents a dragon called Ladon who guarded golden apples in a magical orchard belonging to the goddess Hera. When the warrior Hercules had to steal apples as one of his 12 challenges (see p.73), he killed Ladon. Hera then placed Ladon up in the sky to thank him for serving her.

BOÖTES

With its recognisable kite-like shape and bright orange star at the base, Boötes is an excellent constellation to seek out when the time is right.

THE STATS

Constellation: Boötes
Represents: a herdsman
Visible: Northern Hemisphere and part of the Southern Hemisphere
Best seen: April to June

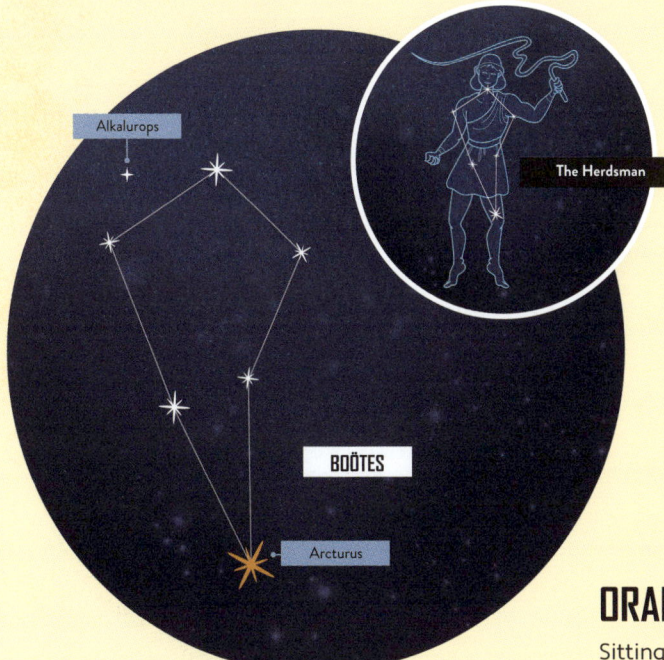

STELLAR TIP

In early January, look to the sky near Boötes, Draco and Hercules and you might just see an impressive light show! The Quadrantids meteor shower comes from this area every year.

ORANGE GLOW

Sitting on the Herdsman's knee is a large star called Arcturus. Arcturus is the fourth-brightest star in the night sky and shines with an orange glow.

STARGAZER CHALLENGE

Use your unaided eyes to locate the star Alkalurops. Now look at this star through your binoculars. Can you see that it is actually two stars close together?

STAR STORY

There are many tales explaining this mysterious farmer in the sky. In Greek, the word *boötes* means 'ox-driver', 'herdsman' or 'ploughman'. He could be herding the nearby bears Ursa Major and Ursa Minor, or pushing the Plough asterism within Ursa Major. In fact, the name of the bright star Arcturus means 'bear-keeper'. However, in some Greek versions of the story, Boötes is another son of Callisto, the nymph who was turned into Ursa Major (see p.64).

NORTHERN HEMISPHERE

CORONA BOREALIS

If you look closely enough, you will see that between the bright Boötes (see p.67) and Hercules (see p.73) sits a regal crown. Search for seven stars in a semicircle shape, like the letter 'U'.

IN AND OUT OF SIGHT

The stars within Corona Borealis vary in brightness, and some of them are quite dim compared to their bright neighbours. One star called T Coronae Borealis is a **variable star** that is usually invisible to the unaided eye. However, every 80 years or so it experiences bursts that make it the brightest star in the constellation for several days, before it dims again for another 80 years!

STARGAZER CHALLENGE

Within the 'U', look for a star called R Coronae Borealis. Instead of brightening intermittently like T Coronae Borealis, this star disappears from view every now and then. Check a stargazer website or app to learn when you might see it.

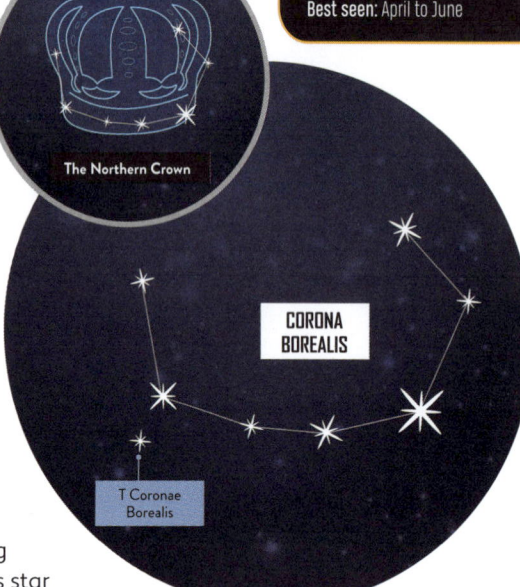

The Northern Crown

CORONA BOREALIS

T Coronae Borealis

THE STATS

Constellation: Corona Borealis
Represents: the northern crown
Visible: Northern Hemisphere and part of the Southern Hemisphere
Best seen: April to June

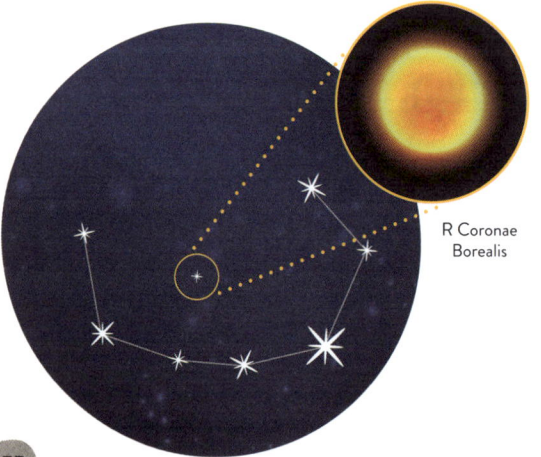

R Coronae Borealis

STAR STORY

In Greek mythology, this crown was given to Ariadne, the Princess of Crete and daughter of King Minos, by Dionysus, the god of fun. When Dionysus asked for Ariadne's hand in marriage, he threw his crown into the sky to prove he was a god. When it stuck in the stars, she accepted his proposal! In Celtic mythology, the constellation is not a crown but a castle. In Native American culture, the shape is a semicircle of tents.

CORONA AUSTRALIS

A similar shape to Corona Borealis shines in the Southern Hemisphere, as the constellation Corona Australis. Some see this constellation as a crown, and others as a boomerang, a bird's nest or a turtle's shell.

THE STATS

Constellation: Corona Australis
Represents: the southern crown
Visible: Southern Hemisphere and part of the Northern Hemisphere
Best seen: June to August

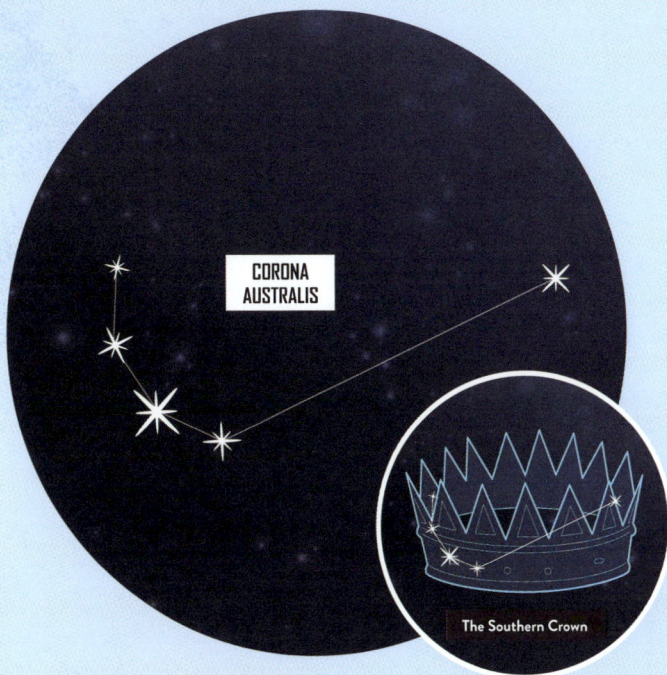

The Southern Crown

SMALL BUT MIGHTY

Corona Australis is one of the smallest constellations in the sky, and its stars are quite dim. Look closely to see a 'U' shape shining between the constellations Scorpius (see p.97) and Sagittarius (see p.98).

STELLAR FACT

Nebulas in the northeastern section of the constellation, next to Sagittarius, dim and brighten with the stars at their cores. These are likely very young stars about to become main sequence stars (see pages 60–61).

STAR STORY

Although its name translates as the 'southern crown', there are many different stories explaining the shape of this cluster of stars. When it was recognised by the Greek astronomer Ptolemy in the second century, it was described as a wreath. To the Chinese, it is a turtle shell, and in Arabic lore it is sometimes described as a bird's nest. In some parts of Australia, people see it as a boomerang. What do you see?

LYRA

This small constellation contains a large wonder: Vega, one of the brightest stars in the sky.

MUSICAL MARVEL

Six stars make up this constellation, which resembles a harp-like musical instrument called a lyre. At the top sparkles Vega, a star that produces over 50 times more light than the Sun. Vega shines with a brilliant blue glow that is visible with the unaided eye.

THE STATS

Constellation: Lyra
Represents: a lyre
Visible: Northern Hemisphere and part of the Southern Hemisphere
Best seen: August to September

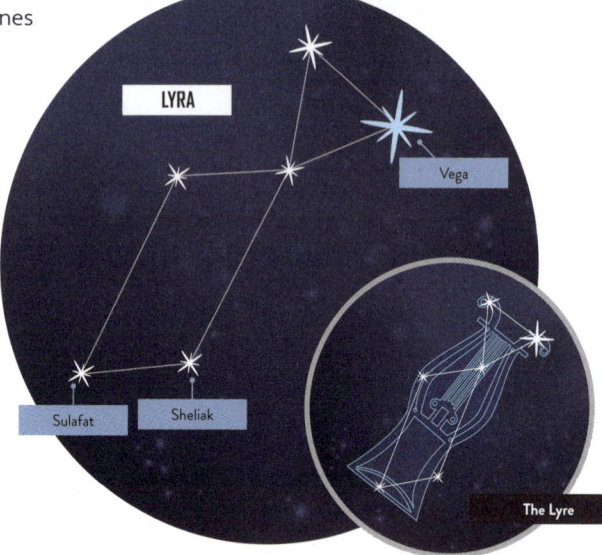

STARGAZER CHALLENGE

Using a small telescope or binoculars, look for the softly glowing Ring Nebula (see p.110) at the bottom of the harp.

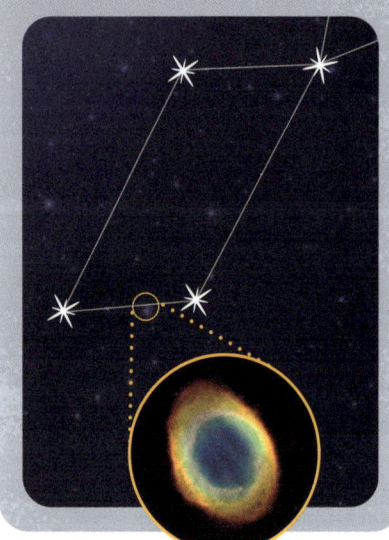

Photograph of the Ring Nebula taken by NASA's Hubble Space Telescope

STAR STORY

In Greek mythology, this lyre belonged to Orpheus, the son of Apollo. When Orpheus's wife Eurydice died, he was so sad that he begged the gods of the underworld to return her to him, using his music to demonstrate his heartbreak. They agreed to do so if Orpheus promised not to look at Eurydice as they left the underworld. He was unable to keep that promise, so Eurydice was returned to the underworld for good. When Orpheus himself died, he and his lyre were placed in the sky by the great god Zeus.

CYGNUS

Soaring across the sky is Cygnus, the great winged swan. Within Cygnus lie an important asterism and another super-bright star.

THE STATS

Constellation: Cygnus
Represents: a swan
Visible: Northern Hemisphere and most of the Southern Hemisphere
Best seen: August and September

NORTHERN CROSS

The stars Deneb, Sadr, Gienah, Delta Cygni and Albireo within this constellation form an asterism called the Northern Cross.

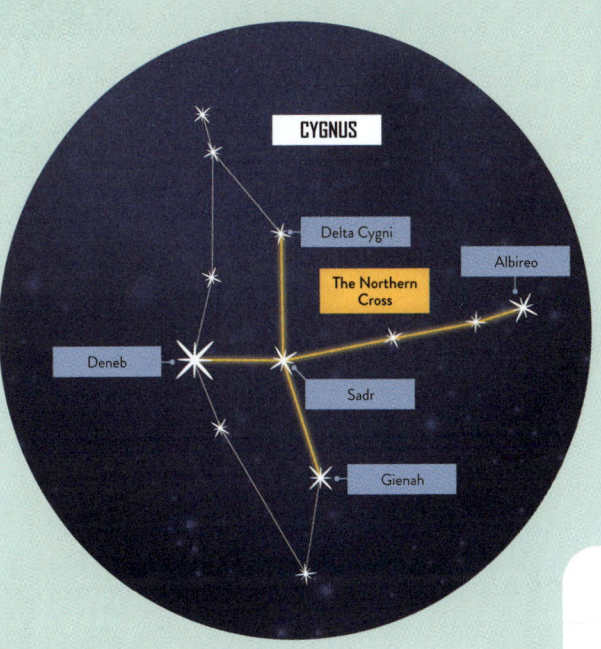

THE SWAN'S TAIL

The brightest star in this constellation is Deneb, an Arabic word that means 'tail'. It forms the tail of the soaring swan.

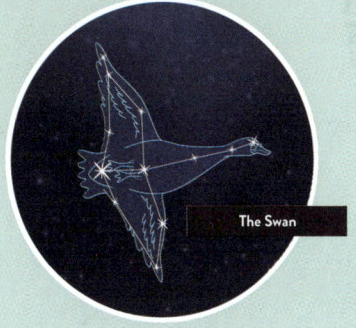

STAR STORY

In Greek mythology, this swan could be Orpheus, placed in the sky alongside his beloved lyre (see p.70). Or it could be Zeus, who turned himself into a swan to attract the queen, Leda. In Chinese mythology, the constellation represents the Magpie Bridge, a crossing made of birds to help two separated lovers come together. In Mongolia, the constellation is recognised as a bow and arrow.

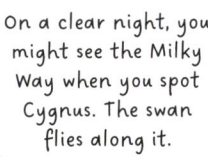

On a clear night, you might see the Milky Way when you spot Cygnus. The swan flies along it.

AQUILA

Flying next to Cygnus the swan (see p.71) is another bird: Aquila the eagle. Look for its large, outstretched wings.

ALTAIR

The eagle's head is formed by Altair, another very bright star. In Arabic, this star's name means 'eagle'. Altair spins so fast that it has a slightly flattened shape.

THE STATS

Constellation: Aquila
Represents: an eagle
Visible: Northern Hemisphere and most of the Southern Hemisphere
Best seen: August to September

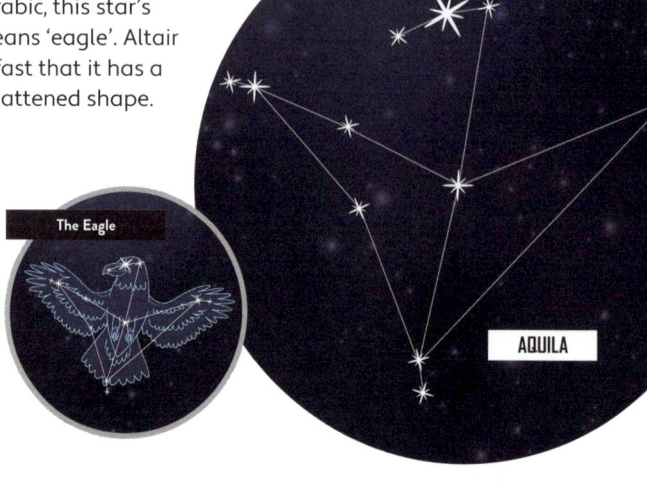

SUMMER TRIANGLE

Along with Vega in Lyra (see p.70) and Deneb in Cygnus (see p.71), Altair is part of an asterism known as the Summer Triangle. In summer in the Northern Hemisphere, it shines overhead, although it can be seen throughout most of the year. In winter in the Southern Hemisphere, this asterism can be seen just above the northern horizon.

STELLAR TIP
Locating the Summer Triangle is a great starting point to lead you to the three linked constellations.

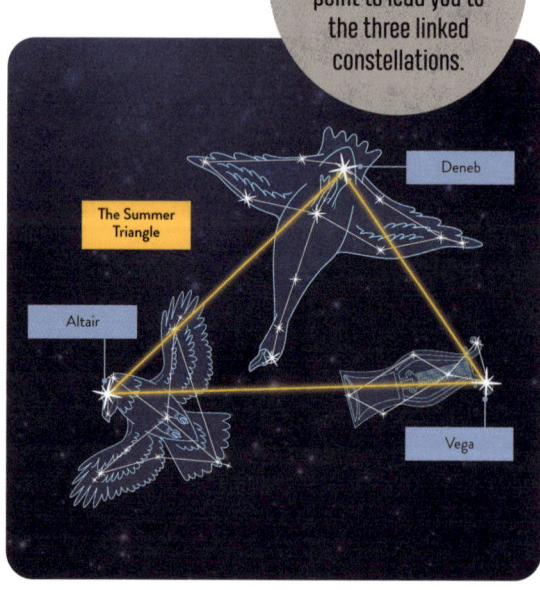

STAR STORY

In one story from Greek mythology, Aquila was the eagle who carried the god Zeus's thunderbolts.

HERCULES

To the Greeks, he was Heracles. To the Romans, he was Hercules. Either way, this great hero is now a large constellation immortalised in the night sky.

> **THE STATS**
>
> **Constellation:** Hercules
> **Represents:** a hero
> **Visible:** both hemispheres at different times
> **Best seen:** April to November (Northern Hemisphere) and June to September (Southern Hemisphere)

THE HERO

Although the stars that form this constellation are not especially bright, the sheer size of the constellation gives the hero his imposing hold on the night sky. Twenty-one stars make up the god's torso, arms, legs and club.

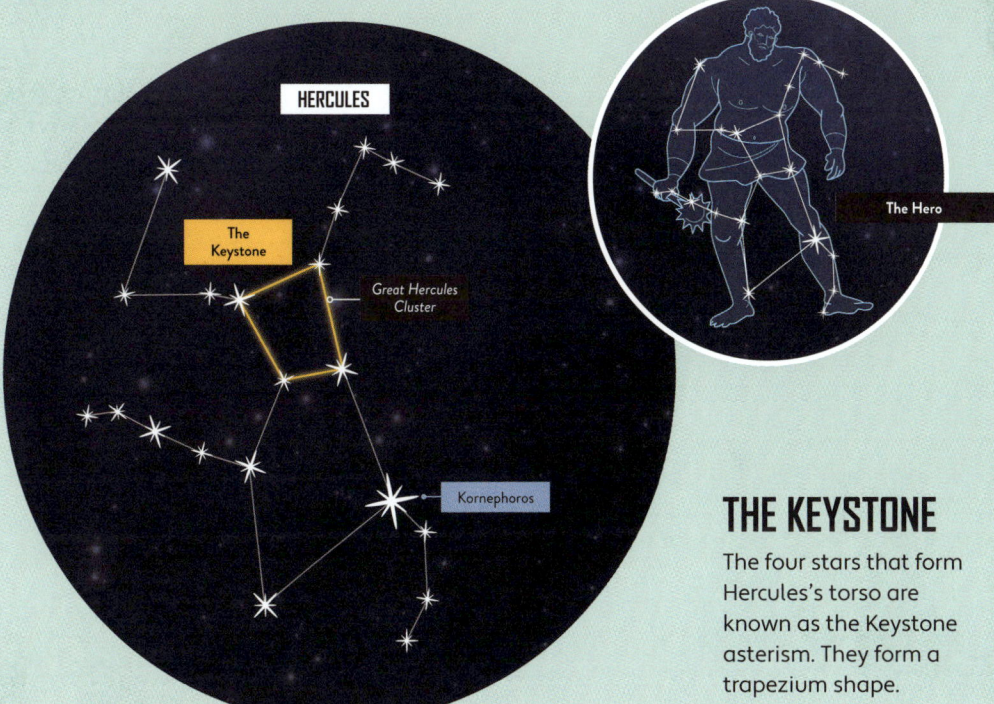

THE KEYSTONE

The four stars that form Hercules's torso are known as the Keystone asterism. They form a trapezium shape.

STAR STORY

Heracles is one of the great heroes of Greek mythology, and was later adapted in Roman mythology to become Hercules. Known for his superhuman strength and bravery, he was forced to undertake 12 nearly impossible tasks. When he completed all 12, the god Zeus (Jupiter in Roman mythology) made him immortal.

PEGASUS

One of the largest constellations in the night sky features another flying creature: a winged horse known as Pegasus.

The Winged Horse

THE STATS

Constellation: Pegasus
Represents: a winged horse
Visible: Northern Hemisphere and most of the Southern Hemisphere
Best seen: July to January (Northern Hemisphere) and August to December (Southern Hemisphere)

THE GREAT SQUARE

To locate Pegasus, first look for an asterism with four stars forming a rough square, known as the Great Square of Pegasus. From there, you can see two front legs, an outstretched neck and a sparkling muzzle.

The winged horse flies the right way up in the Southern Hemisphere, but is upside down in the Northern Hemisphere.

STELLAR TIP

If you move your binoculars or telescope around the inside of the Great Square, you might spot some faint galaxies.

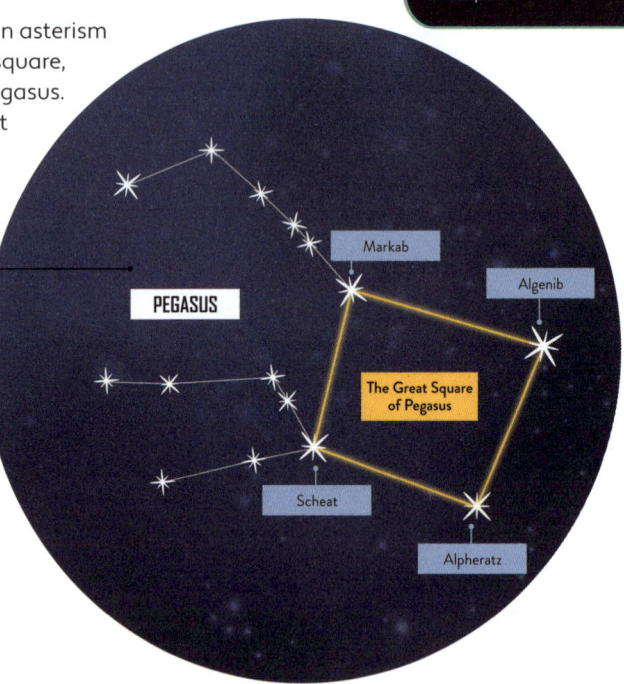

STAR STORY

In Greek mythology, Pegasus was a white winged horse born from the neck of Medusa (see p.75). He created a magical spring called Hippocrene. When anyone drank from this 'horse's fountain', they were given the gift of writing poetry.

PERSEUS

Alongside Pegasus sits the winged horse's rider, the Greek hero Perseus. Another large constellation, this area of the sky holds many exciting secrets.

THE PERSEIDS

Every July and August, Earth passes through the trail of debris left by the Swift-Tuttle comet. As it does, we are treated to a spectacular show of shooting stars. It is known as the Perseid meteor shower because the shooting stars appear to come from the constellation Perseus.

MULTIPLE STARS

Algol (the Arabic for 'demon star') is the second-brightest star in Perseus. It is a variable star, and its brightness changes quite dramatically over a short period of time: just under every three days. This is because it is not one star at all, but three stars revolving around each other! As they revolve, the dimmest star blocks the view of the others from Earth, changing the brightness. Three stars that appear as one in this way are called a triple star. A double star is when two stars appear so close together that they look like one star.

THE STATS

Constellation: Perseus
Represents: a warrior
Visible: Northern Hemisphere and northern parts of the Southern Hemisphere
Best seen: November to December

Double star Pismis 24 in the Scorpius constellation (see p.97), as photographed by the Hubble Space Telescope

STARGAZER CHALLENGE

Observe Perseus over a few clear nights. You should notice that Algol dims and brightens every three days.

STAR STORY

In Greek mythology, it was said that anyone who set their eyes upon the monster Medusa would turn to stone. Perseus defeated Medusa, and her head is represented by the bright star Algol, which Perseus holds in his hand.

ANDROMEDA

Not only does this constellation represent a famous princess in Greek mythology, it is also home to the nearest big galaxy to Earth.

THE STATS

Constellation: Andromeda
Represents: a young woman in chains
Visible: Northern Hemisphere and part of the Southern Hemisphere
Best seen: August to February (Northern Hemisphere) and October to December (Southern Hemisphere)

NEIGHBOURING GALAXY

At the top of one of Andromeda's legs is a fuzzy smudge. This is the Andromeda Galaxy (see p.114), the closest large galaxy to the Milky Way. This spiral galaxy is 2.5 million light-years away, meaning its light takes 2.5 million years to reach Earth.

Andromeda Galaxy

Alpheratz

ANDROMEDA

The Chained Woman

STAR STORY

In Greek mythology, the constellations Cassiopeia (p.79), Perseus (p.75), Pegasus (p.74), Cetus (p.86), Cepheus (p.81) and Andromeda are linked in a dramatic tale. When Andromeda's mother, Queen Cassiopeia of Ethiopia, boasted about her daughter's beauty, the sea god Poseidon became angry and sent a sea monster called Cetus to destroy the kingdom. Queen Cassiopeia and her husband, King Cepheus, offered their daughter as a sacrifice to stop the destruction. Andromeda was chained to rocks but was saved by Perseus flying past on the winged horse Pegasus.

STELLAR TIP

This constellation represents a woman chained to stone. From some locations, she will appear upside down. Look for the bright star Alpheratz, which is one of the corners of the Great Square of Pegasus (see p.74). This forms Andromeda's head.

ORION

In the Northern Hemisphere, winter brings the arrival of Orion and his famous belt in the sky.

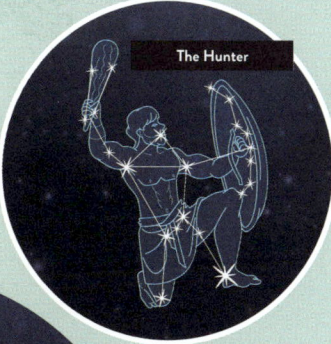
The Hunter

THE STATS

Constellation: Orion
Represents: a hunter
Visible: Northern Hemisphere and most of the Southern Hemisphere
Best seen: January to February

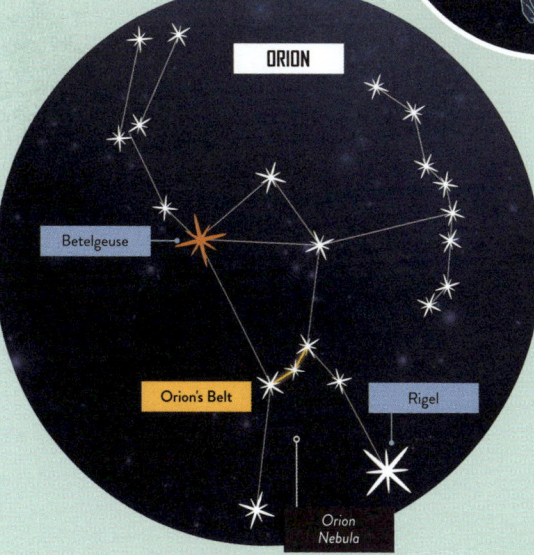

ORION
Betelgeuse
Orion's Belt
Rigel
Orion Nebula

THE HUNTER

A human shape can be seen in these stars. There are two stars forming the shoulders, two at the knees and three bright stars close together in a diagonal line representing the asterism Orion's Belt.

BRIGHT STARS

Betelgeuse and Rigel are two of the brightest stars in the sky, and they are both found in this constellation. Betelgeuse, which has an orangey-red colour, sits at Orion's right shoulder. It is a star in the late stages of its life and will eventually die in an explosion so bright that it will be visible in the daytime. Rigel shines at Orion's left foot.

STAR STORY

In Greek mythology, Orion was a handsome hunter with incredible strength and skill. In some stories, he chases the Seven Sisters (also known as the Pleiades, see p.106) across the sky. In others, he is chased by Scorpius (see p.97), the scorpion that eventually killed him.

Orion Nebula

STARGAZER CHALLENGE

Look below Orion's belt. Can you spot the Orion Nebula (see p.110)?

NORTHERN & SOUTHERN HEMISPHERES

CANIS MAJOR

This constellation is a wonderful sight for amateur stargazers to seek out. Look for the clear shape of a dog, plus the brightest star in the whole night sky!

SIRIUS

On the dog's chest is Sirius, the brightest star in the night sky. If it could be placed next to the Sun, it would shine more than 25 times brighter.

WINTER TRIANGLE

Along with Procyon (see below) and Betelgeuse (see p.77), Sirius forms one of the points of the asterism the Winter Triangle (see p.63). In summer in the Northern Hemisphere, it is high in the sky, while in winter in the Southern Hemisphere, it appears upside down and lower in the sky. If you can find the Winter Triangle, it can help orient you and point you to various constellations.

THE STATS

Constellation: Canis Major
Represents: a big dog
Visible: Southern Hemisphere and most of the Northern Hemisphere
Best seen: January to February

CANIS MINOR

This small dog has many stories – and one very important star!

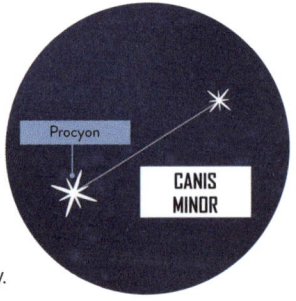

PROCYON

The brightest star in Canis Minor, Procyon is the eighth-brightest star in the night sky. It forms part of the Winter Triangle.

THE STATS

Constellation: Canis Minor
Represents: a small dog
Visible: Southern Hemisphere and most of the Northern Hemisphere
Best seen: January to February

STAR STORY

While in some Greek stories Canis Minor follows Orion around the sky, in others he sits at the feet of Castor and Pollux (see p.95) waiting for scraps of food to fall. In ancient Egypt, the constellation represented the god Anubis, who had the head of a wild dog.

CASSIOPEIA

Sitting on her throne, this Ethiopian queen from Greek mythology rules the northeastern sky.

THE STATS
Constellation: Cassiopeia
Represents: a queen on her throne
Visible: Northern Hemisphere
Best seen: October to November

HOW TO SPOT

Locate the Plough in Ursa Major and follow the pointers up to Polaris (see p.64). Continue following the line until you reach a 'W' or 'M' shape – it changes depending on the time of year and where in the world you are (sometimes even appearing sideways). This is Cassiopeia.

POINTING ARROWS

Once you've found Cassiopeia, it will lead you to other sights in the sky (see p.114). The centre of the 'W' forms an arrow pointing towards Polaris. And if you follow the deep 'V' to the side of this, with bright star Schedar at the tip, you will arrive at the Andromeda Galaxy.

STAR STORY

Look back to page 76 to read Cassiopeia's story.

STELLAR FACT

At the centre of this constellation is a star called Gamma Cassiopeiae. This is a variable star that gets brighter and dimmer unpredictably.

STARGAZER CHALLENGE

Can you spot the foggy band of the Milky Way (see pages 112–113) weaving through Cassiopeia?

Cassiopeia and the Milky Way

NORTHERN HEMISPHERE

AURIGA

In winter in the Northern Hemisphere, Auriga the charioteer drives his chariot through the Milky Way. Look for its bright star to guide you.

THE STATS

Constellation: Auriga
Represents: a charioteer
Visible: Northern Hemisphere and northern parts of the Southern Hemisphere
Best seen: December to February

CAPELLA

The brightest star in the constellation, Capella, shines a bright yellow. Look for the rough shape of the constellation (representing a man and his goats) around this star.

THE WINTER HEXAGON

Along with Rigel from Orion (see p.77), Aldebaran from Taurus (see p.94), Pollux from Gemini (see p.95), Procyon from Canis Minor (see p.78) and Sirius from Canis Major (see p.78), Capella forms one point of the six-sided Winter Hexagon, a recognisable shape visible from the Northern Hemisphere in winter.

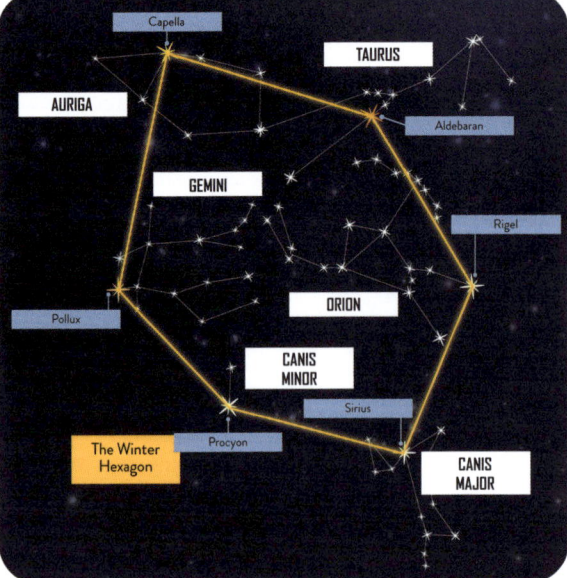

STAR STORY

In Greek mythology, Auriga is often said to represent Erichthonius, the king of Athens and son of the fire god Hephaestus. Erichthonius was the first man to harness four horses to a cart, inventing the chariot on Earth. Islamic astronomers see Auriga as a herd of goats, while the ancient Babylonians saw part of a shepherd's crook.

CEPHEUS

Shaped like a house, this constellation in the northern sky is named after the King of Ethiopia and husband to Cassiopeia (see p.79).

THE STATS

Constellation: Cepheus
Represents: a king
Visible: Northern Hemisphere
Best seen: September to October

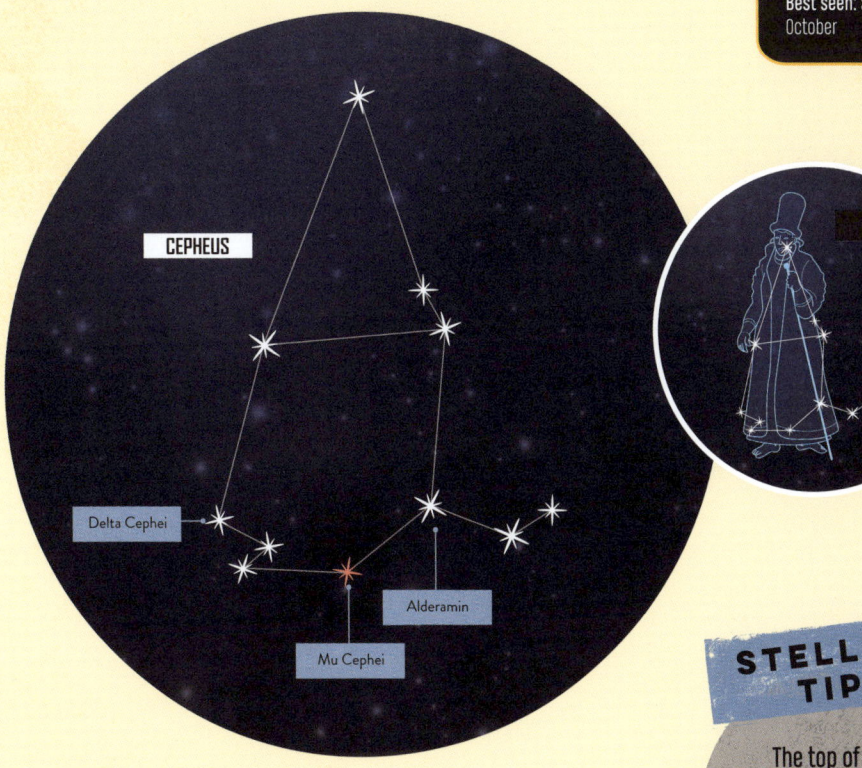

UP NORTH

Cepheus can be found high in the sky in the Northern Hemisphere, circling the North Celestial Pole.

STELLAR TIP

The top of the triangle in Cepheus points towards Polaris, the Pole Star (see p.64).

SUPER STARS

In the bottom-right corner is the brightest star in this constellation: Alderamin. To the left of that is Mu Cephei, a star with a reddish tint. To the left again is Delta Cephei, an important star that helped scientists discover a class of stars called Cepheid variables, which change brightness in a regular pattern.

STAR STORY

Look back to page 76 to read the story of Cepheus.

HYDRA

The longest constellation of all, Hydra covers more sky than any of the other 87 constellations.

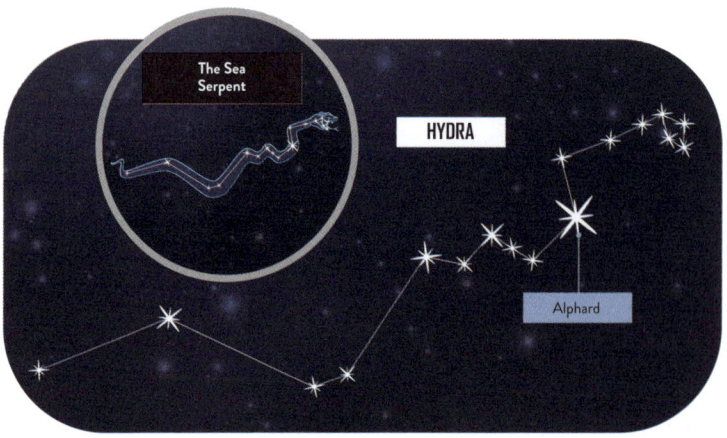

THE STATS

Constellation: Hydra
Represents: a sea serpent
Visible: Southern Hemisphere and parts of the Northern Hemisphere
Best seen: January to May

RECORD BREAKER

Hydra covers 100 degrees of the sky – more than half of the area you can see! The sea serpent stretches from Libra in the south (see p.97) to Cancer in the north (see p.95).

HOW TO SPOT

Although this constellation is large, it isn't especially bright. Look for it on a clear night in the first half of the year. Search for the bright star Alphard at the serpent's heart, then follow the line of stars out in each direction from there.

STAR STORY

In Greek mythology, Heracles (Hercules in Roman mythology, see p.73) was tasked with defeating this sea monster as one of his 12 labours. Whenever Heracles cut off one head, another two grew back! However, the constellation shows only one head on the serpent.

STARGAZER CHALLENGE

Use binoculars to spot the Southern Pinwheel Galaxy (M83) near Hydra's tail. With a telescope, you might even be able to make out its spiral shape.

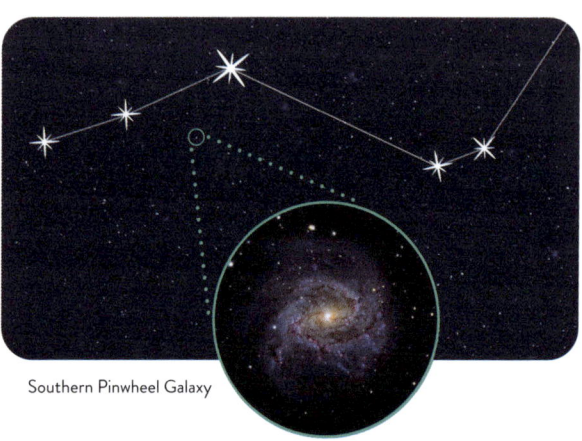

Southern Pinwheel Galaxy

HYDRUS

Unlike Hydra (see p.82), Hydrus is a small constellation, visible mostly from the Southern Hemisphere.

SMALLER SNAKE

While Hydra is the large sea serpent, Hydrus is the much smaller water snake. It circles the South Celestial Pole.

THE STATS

Constellation: Hydrus
Represents: a water snake
Visible: Southern Hemisphere and southern parts of the Northern Hemisphere
Best seen: October to December

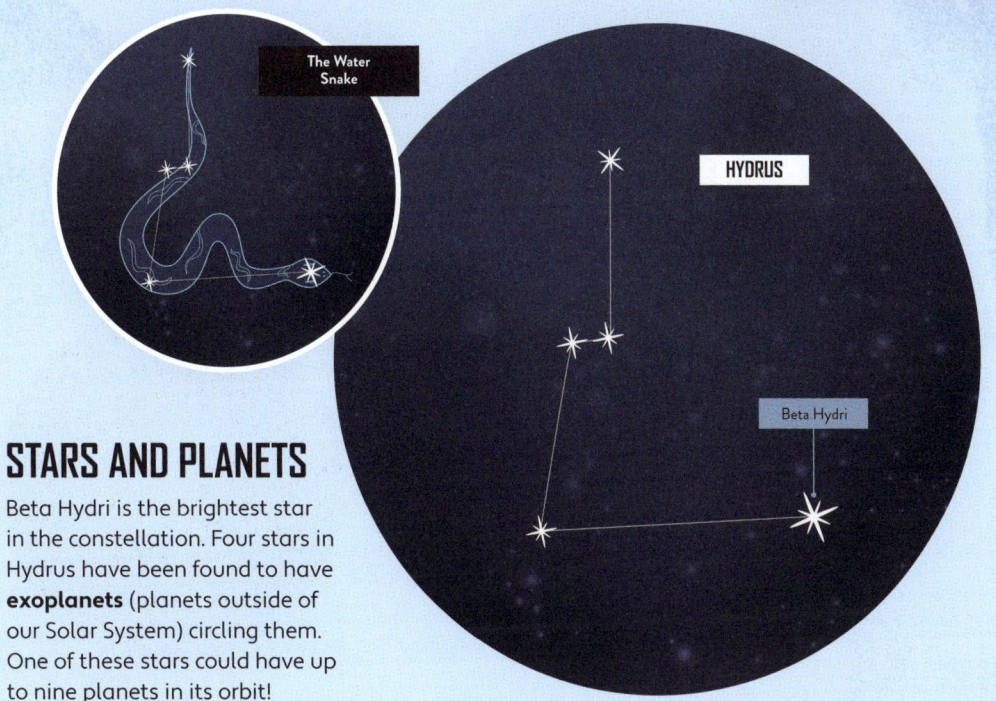

The Water Snake

HYDRUS

Beta Hydri

STARS AND PLANETS

Beta Hydri is the brightest star in the constellation. Four stars in Hydrus have been found to have **exoplanets** (planets outside of our Solar System) circling them. One of these stars could have up to nine planets in its orbit!

Snakes in the sky!

STAR STORY

In the late 1500s, Dutch astronomer Petrus Plancius named 12 constellations in the Southern Hemisphere. Many of these represented what Dutch sailors and explorers saw on their travels. Hydrus was inspired by the water snakes they spotted.

TUCANA

One of a group of constellations known as the 'southern birds', Tucana the toucan perches above the Southern Hemisphere, although it can be seen from southern parts of the Northern Hemisphere. The brightest star, Alpha Tucanae, forms the toucan's beak.

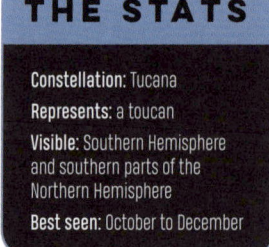

THE STATS

Constellation: Tucana
Represents: a toucan
Visible: Southern Hemisphere and southern parts of the Northern Hemisphere
Best seen: October to December

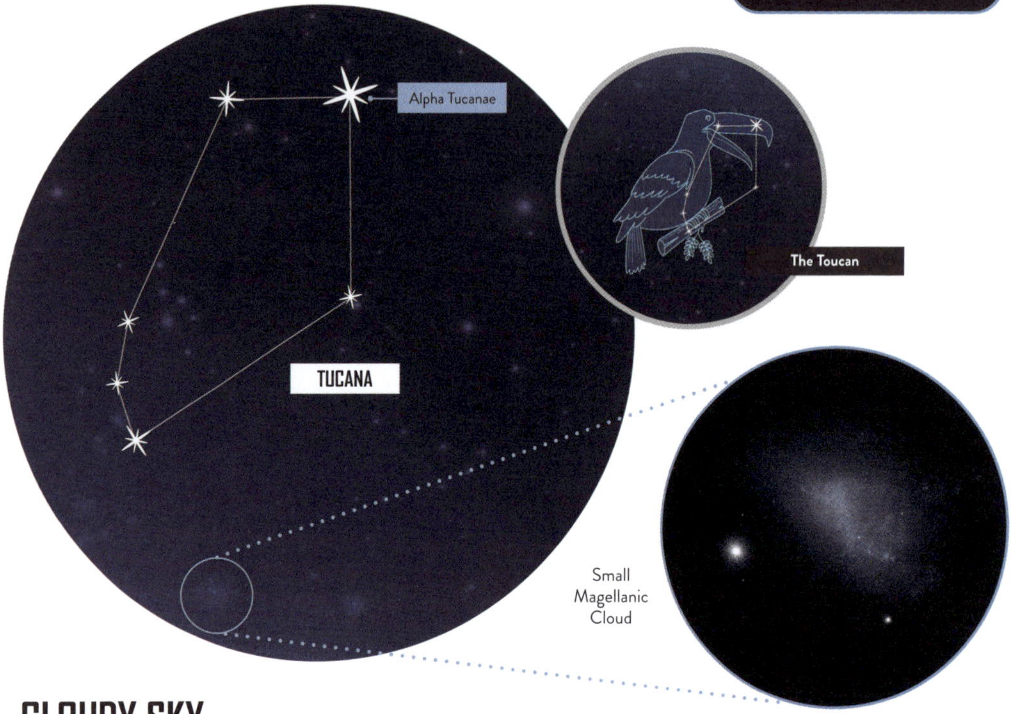

CLOUDY SKY

The Tucana constellation is home to the Small Magellanic Cloud (see p.115). This small galaxy can be seen as a misty smudge with the unaided eye.

STAR STORY

Tucana the toucan is another one of the constellations named by Dutch mapmaker Petrus Plancius in the late 1500s (see p.83). His 12 constellations included other animals, such as Pavo the peacock, Grus the crane and Hydrus the water snake (see p.83).

STELLAR FACT: Some people think Tucana looks like the shape of a simple boat in the sky.

CENTAURUS

Centaurus is one of the largest and brightest constellations in the southern sky. Within it, you can discover many special celestial objects.

THE STATS

Constellation: Centaurus
Represents: a centaur (half-human, half-horse)
Visible: Southern Hemisphere and southern parts of the Northern Hemisphere
Best seen: May

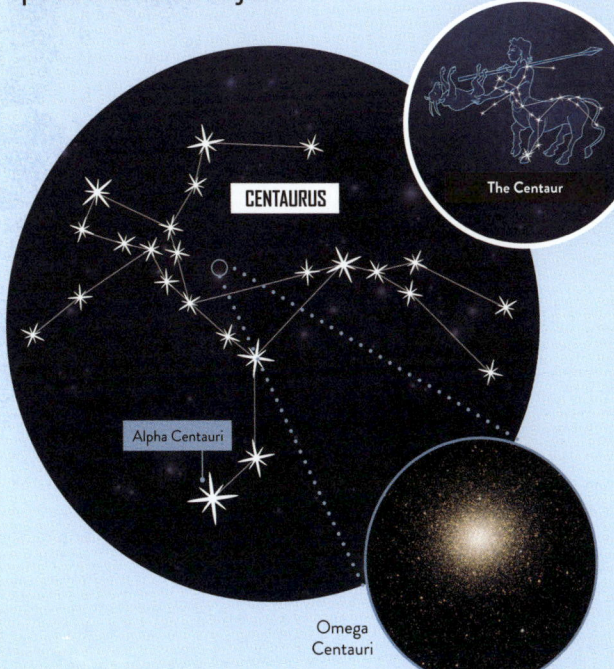

SOUTHERN SIGHT

Seen mainly from the Southern Hemisphere, this constellation is a landmark in the southern sky, helping sailors to orient themselves.

STELLAR FACT

The brightest star in the constellation, Alpha Centauri, is actually three stars close together. One of these, Proxima Centauri, is the closest star to Earth, after the Sun. It is 4.25 light years away, meaning that its light takes 4.25 years to reach us.

CLUSTER OF STARS

An enormous star cluster called Omega Centauri (see p.107) shines in Centaurus. It is the largest **globular cluster** (see pages 104–105) in the Milky Way and contains about 10 million stars.

STARGAZER CHALLENGE

Find a very dark area to stargaze. Can you spot Omega Centauri with just your eyes? It should look like a sparkly patch about the size of a full moon.

STAR STORY

To the Greeks, this constellation represented a centaur: a creature that is half-human and half-horse. To the Babylonians, it was a bison with four animal legs and a human head and torso.

CETUS

Known as the sea monster or the whale, Cetus swims in the sea of the night sky.

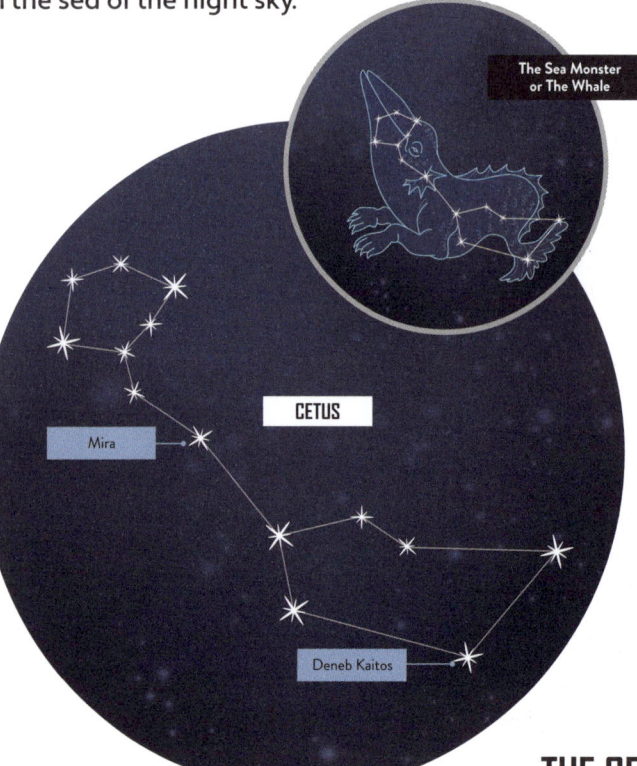

The Sea Monster or The Whale

CETUS
Mira
Deneb Kaitos

THE STATS

Constellation: Cetus
Represents: a whale or sea monster
Visible: Southern Hemisphere and southern parts of the Northern Hemisphere
Best seen: November

HOW TO SPOT

Start by locating the Great Square of Pegasus (see p.74). Draw an imaginary line from Alpheratz to Algenib. Continue the line and you will reach Deneb Kaitos, the brightest star in Cetus. This star's name means 'the whale's tail'.

THE SEA OF THE HEAVENS

Cetus lives in an area of the sky known as the Sea of the Heavens, or the Heavenly Waters. Other watery constellations share this home, such as Piscis Austrinus the fish (see p.91) and Delphinus the dolphin.

STAR STORY

According to Greek legend, Cetus represents the sea monster defeated by Perseus in order to save the beautiful Andromeda (see p.76). To the ancient Romans, it might have been modelled on the shape of an actual whale skeleton.

STELLAR FACT

The star Mira in this constellation was the first variable star to be named by astronomers. Sometimes it gets so dim that it disappears to the unaided eye before brightening again. Its name comes from the word 'miracle' or 'miraculous'.

CARINA

Another constellation in the southern sky with a seafaring theme, Carina represents the keel of a ship: the structure along its base that supports the ship as a whole.

SHOWING THE WAY

Like many constellations, Carina helped sailors to find their way. It shines brightly near the South Celestial Pole and is home to the Carina Nebula (see p.33 and p.111), where many stars are formed.

THE STATS

Constellation: Carina
Represents: a ship's keel
Visible: Southern Hemisphere and southern parts of the Northern Hemisphere
Best seen: March

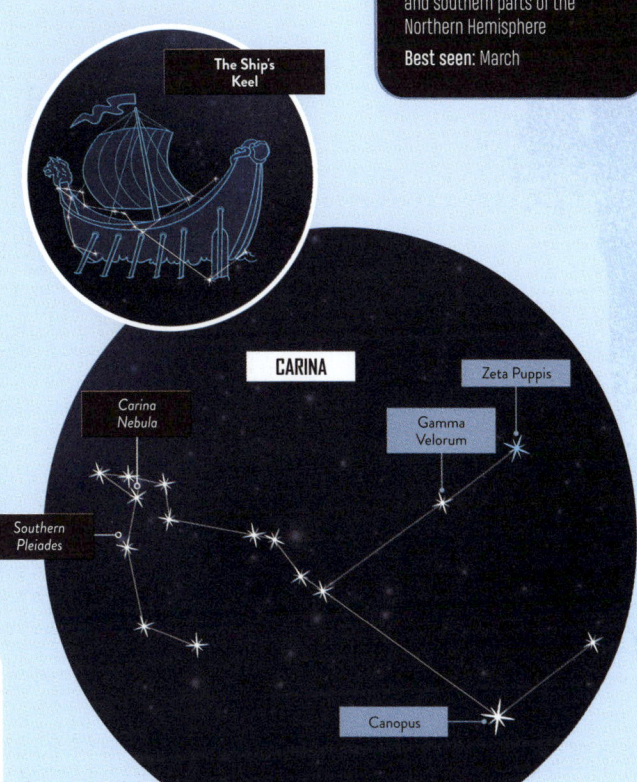

BRIGHT STAR

Carina's brightest star, Canopus, is the second-brightest star in the night sky as viewed from Earth. However, if it were placed next to the Sun, it would shine more than 13,000 times brighter!

STAR STORY

Carina was once part of a larger constellation called Argo Navis, which represented a ship called *Argo*. This ship was used by the Greek hero Jason and his crew on a quest to steal the magical Golden Fleece. In 1763, French astronomer Nicolas-Louis de Lacaille split the constellation into three smaller ones. Carina remains as the ship's keel.

STARGAZER CHALLENGE

Look to the side of the ship's base. Can you spot the sparkling Southern Pleiades star cluster (see p.106)?

STELLAR FACT

In the 19th century, the variable star Eta Carinae, found in the Carina Nebula, shone even brighter than Canopus.

VELA

Along with Carina (see p.87) and Puppis (see p.89), Vela once formed part of the larger Argo Navis ship constellation.

THE STATS

Constellation: Vela
Represents: a ship's sails
Visible: Southern Hemisphere and most of the Northern Hemisphere
Best seen: March

QUADRUPLE STAR

Vela's brightest star, Gamma Velorum, is actually at least four stars that appear close together. It is also known by the name Regor.

LIGHTHOUSE IN THE SKY

When a giant star exploded in the Vela constellation about 10,000 years ago, it formed a dense object called the Vela Pulsar, which emits charged particles. This object rotates 11 times every second – faster than a helicopter rotor! As it spins, it brightens and flashes like a lighthouse.

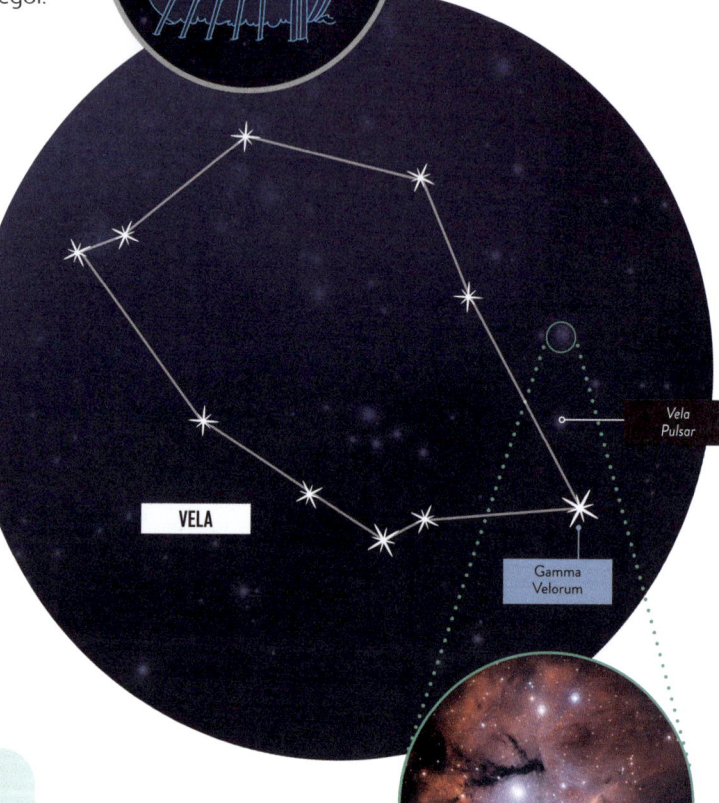

The Ship's Sails

Vela Pulsar

VELA

Gamma Velorum

Gum Nebula

STAR STORY

Look back to page 87 to read the story of the *Argo* ship. Vela represents the ship's sails.

GREAT GUM

This part of the sky is home to the huge Gum Nebula. It was named after Colin S. Gum, the astronomer who discovered it.

PUPPIS

Completing the original Argo Navis ship constellation (see p.87) is Puppis, the stern or rear.

THE STATS

Constellation: Puppis
Represents: a ship's stern
Visible: Southern Hemisphere and most of the Northern Hemisphere
Best seen: February to March

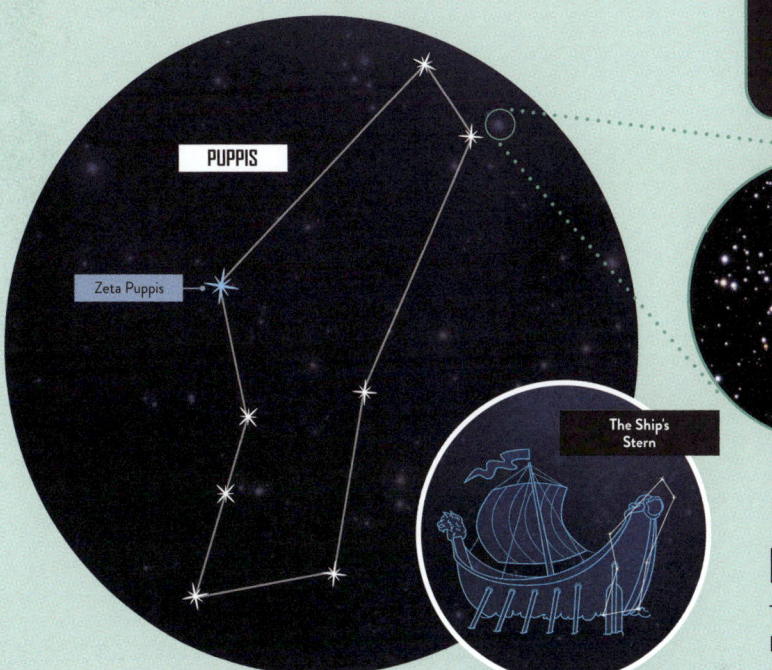

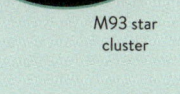

M93 star cluster

BRIGHT BLUE

The brightest star in Puppis is Zeta Puppis, which also happens to be the brightest and nearest blue supergiant to Earth.

HOW TO SPOT

Look for Puppis low on the southern horizon. First find Sirius in Canis Major (see p.78). Draw an imaginary line from Sirius to Adhara (also in Canis Major) and continue this line until you reach Puppis.

STAR STORY

Read the story of the *Argo* ship on page 87. Puppis takes the shape of the stern at the back of the ship.

STARGAZER CHALLENGE

Using a telescope, can you spot the M93 star cluster at the top of the stern?

ERIDANUS

Weaving through the southern skies is Eridanus, the winding river. This constellation is the sixth-largest of all.

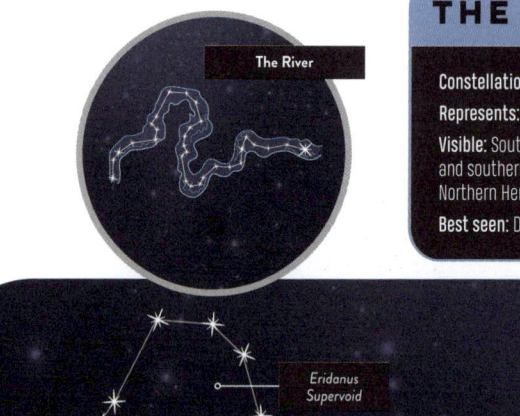

THE STATS

Constellation: Eridanus
Represents: a river
Visible: Southern Hemisphere and southern parts of the Northern Hemisphere
Best seen: December

WINDING RIVER

The river begins near Rigel in the constellation Orion (see p.77). From there, it meanders through the southern sky all the way along to its brightest star, Achernar.

FLAT STAR

In Arabic, bright star Achernar's name means 'end of the river'. As you might guess, it sits at one end of the constellation. It is one of the flattest stars known. It spins so fast that its middle bulges out. This star is visible only from the Southern Hemisphere.

STAR STORY

This constellation might take its name from Eridu, a city in ancient Babylon.

STELLAR FACT

In the middle of the Eridanus constellation is the Eridanus Supervoid. Discovered in 2007, this large, dark region has barely any stars or galaxies at all.

Eridanus Supervoid

SOUTHERN HEMISPHERE

90

PISCIS AUSTRINUS

Not to be confused with Pisces (see p.99), the constellation of Piscis Austrinus also represents a fish. Its name means 'southern fish'.

THE STATS

Constellation: Piscis Austrinus
Represents: the southern fish
Visible: Southern Hemisphere and parts of the Northern Hemisphere
Best seen: September and October

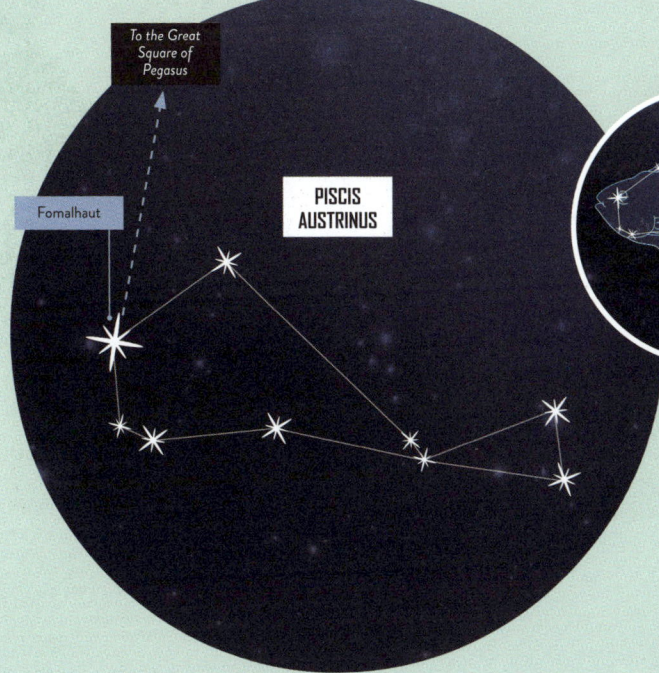

The Southern Fish

FISH MOUTH

The brightest star in this constellation is Fomalhaut, which means 'mouth of the fish'. It is the 18th-brightest star that can be seen with the unaided eye.

HOW TO SPOT

First locate the Great Square of Pegasus (see p.74). Draw an imaginary line from Scheat towards Markab and keep going until you reach Fomalhaut in Piscis Austrinus. This star stays close to the horizon all year long.

STAR STORY

In Greek mythology, Piscis Austrinus is the Great Fish. The Greeks saw it drinking water poured by Aquarius, the water bearer, and said that the two fish in the Pisces constellation were its children (see p.99). In ancient Babylonia, this constellation was the large fish that rescued the Syrian goddess Atargatis from a lake.

THE ZODIAC

While constellations are found across the entire night sky, 12 of them sit along the ecliptic, the path the Sun appears to follow through the sky (see p.29). These 12 constellations are grouped into a special set called the Zodiac. You can see them from both the Northern and Southern Hemispheres.

SOLAR VISITOR

Because of the way the Sun and Earth move in space, the Sun appears to travel through the sky (although we know that, really, it's us that's moving!). Over the course of one year, the Sun appears to move past each of these special constellations, spending about a month in the section of sky belonging to each set of stars.

STARRY DESTINY

Some people believe that where the Sun was in the sky on the day you were born affects your personality and your life. However, the Sun and Earth wobble on their axes, so the position of the Zodiac constellations has shifted over time and no longer matches up with the dates for each star sign.

ASTROLOGY OR ASTRONOMY?

While astronomy is the scientific study of the stars, astrology is the belief that their position can affect human characteristics and behaviour. Astrologists study the movements of celestial bodies and how they affect humans and the natural world.

ARIES

The first sign of the Zodiac, Aries marked the beginning of spring and the start of a new year to people in the Northern Hemisphere thousands of years ago.

The Ram

THE STATS

Constellation: Aries
Represents: a ram
Visible: along the ecliptic (Northern and Southern Hemispheres)
Best seen: November to December

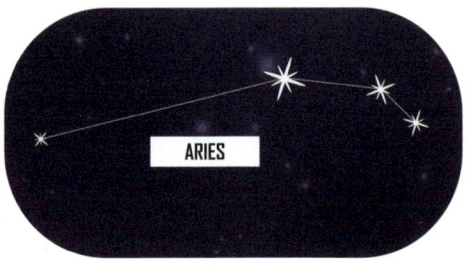
ARIES

STAR STORY

In Greek mythology, Aries is the ram (male sheep) that provided the magical Golden Fleece stolen by Jason and the Argonauts.

TAURUS

Within this second constellation of the Zodiac, many wonders are to be found.

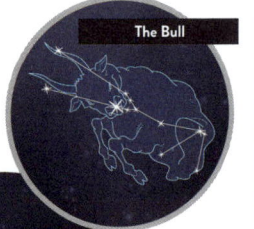
The Bull

THE STATS

Constellation: Taurus
Represents: a bull
Visible: along the ecliptic (Northern and Southern Hemispheres)
Best seen: January to February

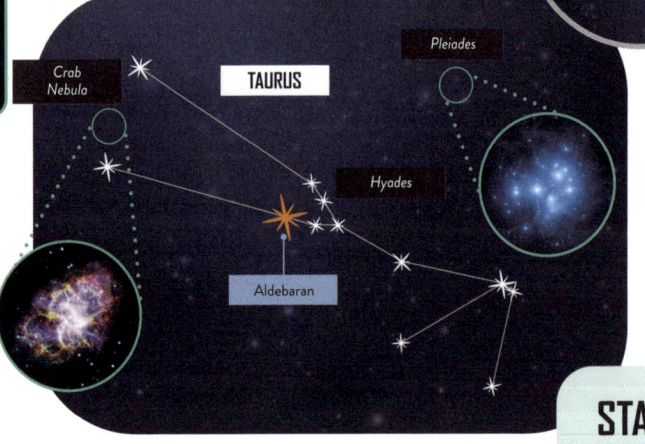

LOTS TO SPOT

The head of this bull is made up of a star cluster called the Hyades. Another famous star cluster, the Pleiades (see p.106), is also found in Taurus, as is the Crab Nebula (see p.111).

ALDEBARAN

The brightest star in this constellation, Aldebaran, is a star nearing the end of its life. It appears as a reddish-orange colour.

STAR STORY

According to Greek legend, the god Zeus turned into a bull to attract a woman named Europa. He carried her on his back all the way to the continent that is now called Europe.

GEMINI

In this one constellation live two figures known as the twins, or *Gemini* in ancient Greek.

THE TWINS

The two brightest stars form the heads of the twins, and give the twins their names too. They are named Castor and Pollux.

STELLAR TIP

Castor appears a bluish-white colour, while Pollux looks orange.

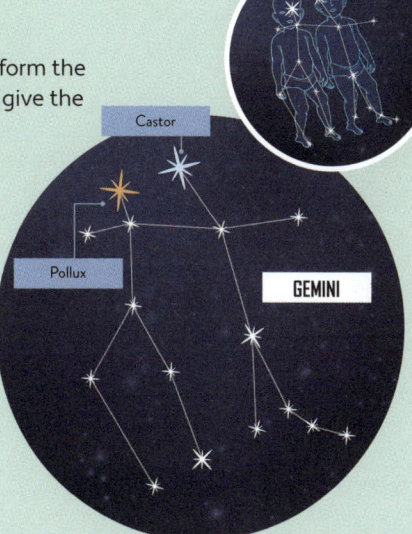

THE STATS

Constellation: Gemini
Represents: the twins
Visible: along the ecliptic (Northern and Southern Hemispheres)
Best seen: February to March

STAR STORY

Though they were twins, Castor and Pollux were very different. In Greek mythology, Pollux was immortal, while Castor was not. When Castor was killed in battle, Pollux gave up his own immortality to be with his brother. Both twins were placed in the sky together.

CANCER

If you're looking for a challenge, try to find the constellation of Cancer. With its faint stars, it is tricky to spot. Look carefully and you should see the Beehive Cluster (see p.106) too.

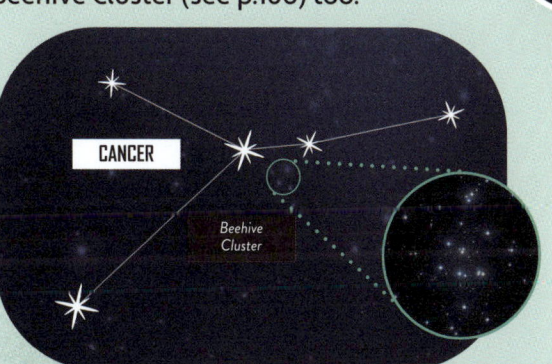

THE STATS

Constellation: Cancer
Represents: a crab
Visible: along the ecliptic (Northern and Southern Hemispheres)
Best seen: March to April

STAR STORY

In Greek mythology, Hera sent the crab to rescue Hydra from Heracles (see p.82). Although the crab did not succeed, Hera placed it in the sky to thank it for its efforts.

LEO

In a fairly empty section of sky, the great beast Leo the lion reigns supreme.

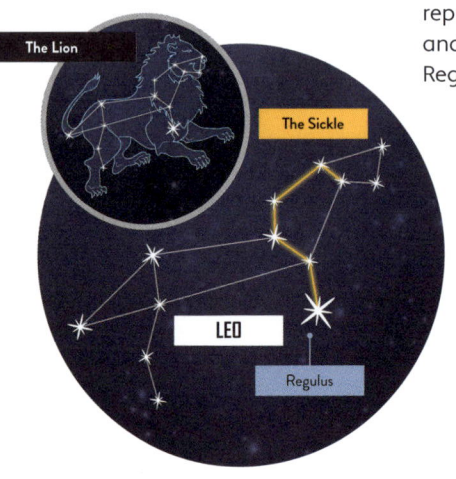

REGAL REGULUS

Look for a backwards question mark to identify this constellation. This asterism is called the Sickle and represents the lion's head and neck. The brightest star, Regulus, sits at the bottom.

THE STATS

Constellation: Leo
Represents: a lion
Visible: along the ecliptic (Northern and Southern Hemispheres)
Best seen: March to April

STAR STORY

In Greek mythology, Leo represents the lion killed by Heracles (see p.73). To ancient Egyptians, it was a sphinx with a lion's body and human head. In other cultures, this group of stars is seen as a horse or a mountain lion.

VIRGO

This mysterious young woman is the largest constellation of the Zodiac and the second-largest constellation in the sky.

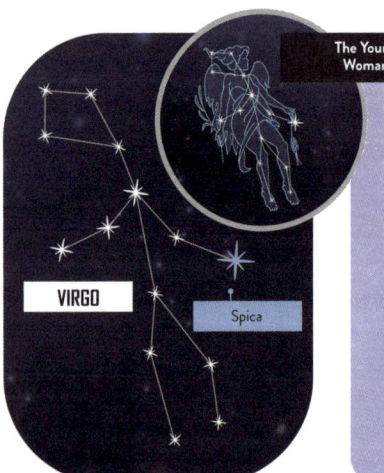

SPICA

Virgo is a faint constellation, but its brightest star Spica stands out. Spica is actually a double star that appears bright blue.

THE STATS

Constellation: Virgo
Represents: a young woman
Visible: along the ecliptic (Northern and Southern Hemispheres)
Best seen: May to June

HOW TO SPOT

The saying goes, 'Arc to Arcturus and speed on to Spica'. Start at the Plough (see p.64). Follow its curved handle in an arc towards the bright star Arcturus (see p.67). From there continue the arc south to Spica.

STAR STORY

There are different ideas of who this woman could be. In Greek mythology she might have been Demeter, the harvest goddess. To the ancient Babylonians, she was a goddess of fertility and family called Ishtar.

LIBRA

This small and faint constellation is the only one of the Zodiac that does not represent a living creature.

THE STATS

Constellation: Libra
Represents: a set of scales
Visible: along the ecliptic (Northern and Southern Hemispheres)
Best seen: June to July

HOW TO SPOT

Find Antares in Scorpius (below). Draw a straight line from there to Spica in Virgo (see p.96). Sitting in the centre of that line will be Libra. Look for the telltale triangle of the three brightest stars at the top.

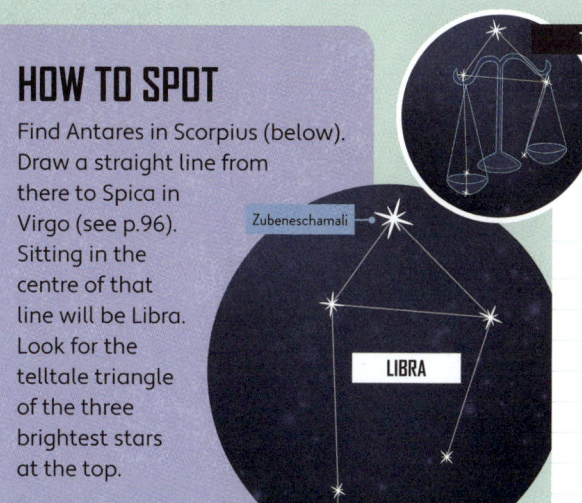

The Scales

Zubeneschamali

LIBRA

STAR STORY

In Latin, Libra means 'weighing scales'. To the ancient Babylonians, the constellation represented a set of scales and balance. However, to ancient Greek and Arab astronomers, the constellation formed the claws of Scorpius (see below). The name of the brightest star, Zubeneschamali, means 'northern claw'.

SCORPIUS

A long, curving string of bright stars forms the shape of Scorpius the scorpion in the night sky.

The Scorpion

Antares

SCORPIUS

Scorpius also goes by the name Scorpio.

THE STATS

Constellation: Scorpius
Represents: a scorpion
Visible: along the ecliptic (Northern and Southern Hemispheres)
Best seen: July to August

RED HEART

A reddish star named Antares shines brightly as the scorpion's heart. Antares is a red supergiant (see pages 60–61). Placed next to our Sun, it would measure about 300 times wider and look 10,000 times brighter!

STAR STORY

In the Greek legend, Scorpius is the scorpion that defeated the hunter Orion with its deadly sting (see p.77). The two constellations now chase each other around the sky.

SAGITTARIUS

Aiming at the heart of the Scorpion (see p.97), Sagittarius the archer holds his bow and arrow high.

Sagittarius A*

THE STATS

Constellation: Sagittarius
Represents: an archer
Visible: along the ecliptic (Northern and Southern Hemispheres)
Best seen: August to September

SAGITTARIUS A*

At the centre of the Milky Way is a black hole: a small area in space with a gravitational pull so strong that nothing can escape – not even light. This black hole lies in the region of the Sagittarius constellation and is known as Sagittarius A*.

TEATIME

Within this constellation is an asterism of eight stars known as the Teapot.

CAPRICORNUS

Many years ago, the sight of Capricornus signalled the start of winter in the Northern Hemisphere, when the Sun would appear in the middle of the Sea Goat.

Capricornus also goes by the name Capricorn.

THE STATS

Constellation: Capricornus
Represents: a sea goat (half-goat, half-fish)
Visible: along the ecliptic (Northern and Southern Hemispheres)
Best seen: August to September

STAR STORY

According to Greek mythology, Pan was a god who changed himself into a goat-fish so that he could jump into the River Nile to escape a giant. In ancient Mesopotamia, the constellation instead represents the water god Ea.

STARGAZER CHALLENGE

At one of the pointed corners you will find the star Algedi. Can you see that it is in fact two stars very close together?

NORTHERN & SOUTHERN HEMISPHERES

AQUARIUS

This constellation represents a large figure carrying water. Can you spot the stars that make up the jug?

THE STATS

Constellation: Aquarius
Represents: a water bearer
Visible: along the ecliptic (Northern and Southern Hemispheres)
Best seen: September to October

HOW TO SPOT

While Aquarius is quite large, it is also fairly faint, so it takes patience to find it in the sky. First, look for the Pegasus constellation (see p.74). Aquarius lies below it. You can also search for the arrow shape of the Water Jug asterism to be sure you're in the right place.

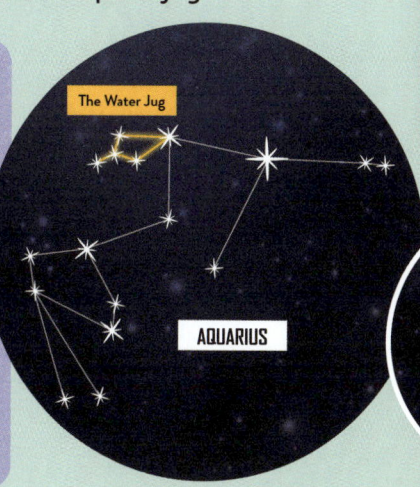

PISCES

The final constellation of the Zodiac, Pisces represents not one but two small fish, joined together by a string of stars.

THE STATS

Constellation: Pisces
Represents: a pair of fish
Visible: along the ecliptic (Northern and Southern Hemispheres)
Best seen: October to November

SWIMMING IN THE SKY

The cord joining the two fish forms a 'V' shape in the night sky. At the point of the V is the constellation's brightest star, Alrisha. A small circle of stars forms the larger of the two fish. This is known as the Circlet asterism.

STAR STORY

In Greek mythology, the two fish represent the goddess Aphrodite and her son Eros. To escape a monster called Typhon, Aphrodite and Eros tied themselves together with rope, turned themselves into fish and jumped into a river. However, the Babylonians in ancient Mesopotamia viewed this constellation as a swallow.

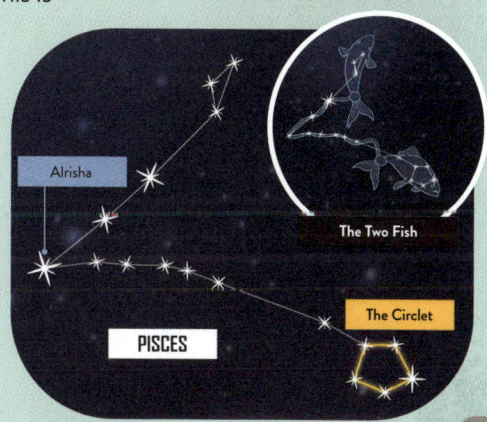

CREATE A CONSTELLATION!

Make up a constellation of your own! Study the stars, find your own patterns and tell their stories.

YOU WILL NEED:
* A notebook
* A pencil
* A red-light torch

STELLAR TIP

Remember to use your red-light torch if you need to see your paper!

The Paintbrush

The Painter

STEP 1
SKETCH THE STARS

Go outside on a clear, warm, dark night. Wait for your eyes to adjust to get the best view of the night sky. In your notebook, sketch the stars that you see.

STEP 2
NAME A CONSTELLATION

What patterns can you see? Join the dots to create shapes of people, animals or objects in the stars on your page. Give your constellation a name!

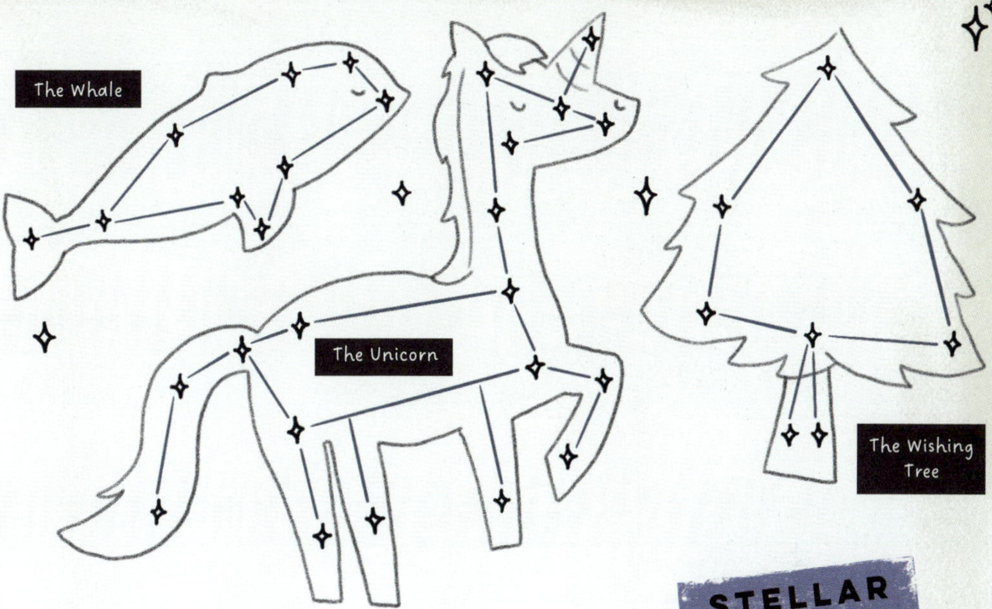

The Whale

The Unicorn

The Wishing Tree

STEP 3 TELL A STORY

In your notebook, write the star story for your constellation. What does the pattern represent? Where did it come from? How did the person, animal or object get in the sky, and why?

STELLAR TIP

So that you – and others! – can find it again, note your location and the best time of night and year to spot your constellation.

STARGAZER CHALLENGE

Are there any special features that can help people find your constellation? Look for bright stars or small groups of stars that form their own shape (asterism) within the constellation. You could even give these stars and asterisms names.

101

CHAPTER FIVE

NIGHT-SKY SPOTTER

We've studied the planets and stars, and discovered their secrets and stories. But there are many other wonders to see in the night sky! In this chapter, you'll learn about star clusters, nebulas and galaxies – what they are and what you might be able to spot for yourself. Look closely at the information and images in this guide, then journey into the night once again to seek them out.

LET'S GO!

STAR CLUSTERS

Many stars are spread out across the night sky, but some are quite close together. Groups of stars are called star clusters. There are two types: globular clusters and open clusters.

Many globular clusters look like a hazy patch of light to the unaided eye. Powerful telescopes will give you the best view.

GLOBULAR CLUSTERS

Large groups of stars are called globular clusters. They can have anywhere from several thousand to several million stars. These stars are packed together in a sphere shape, held together by gravity. Many of the stars in these clusters are billions of years old – some of the oldest in the galaxy!

Messier 13 (M13), also known as the Great Hercules Cluster, can be found in the constellation of Hercules (see p.73).

STELLAR FACT

The Milky Way is surrounded by an area of gas and stars called the galactic halo. Most globular clusters are found here.

104

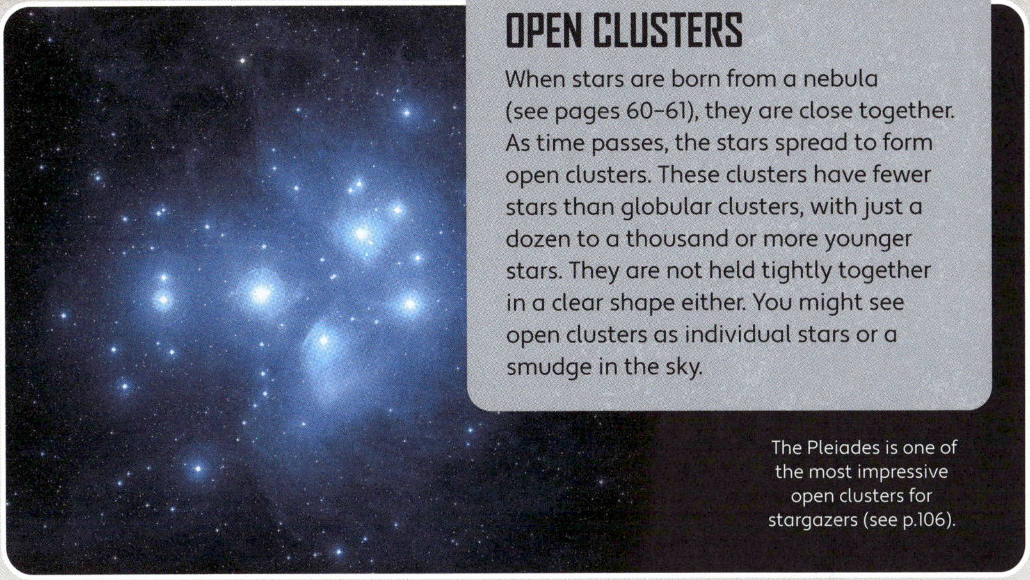

The Pleiades

OPEN CLUSTERS

When stars are born from a nebula (see pages 60–61), they are close together. As time passes, the stars spread to form open clusters. These clusters have fewer stars than globular clusters, with just a dozen to a thousand or more younger stars. They are not held tightly together in a clear shape either. You might see open clusters as individual stars or a smudge in the sky.

The Pleiades is one of the most impressive open clusters for stargazers (see p.106).

SPOTTING CLUSTERS

Some star clusters can be seen with the unaided eye, while others require binoculars or a telescope. Turn the page for special clusters to seek out.

STELLAR FACT

The first globular star cluster was recorded in 1665, when it could be clearly spotted following the invention of the telescope.

The Double Cluster in Perseus (see p.75) is visible to the unaided eye in the right conditions, but you'll get a better view through binoculars.

105

THE BEEHIVE

On a dark night, the Beehive Cluster appears as a faint, fuzzy object about three times wider than the Moon. Use binoculars or a telescope to make out some of the glittering stars within it.

The Beehive Cluster as seen through a telescope

THE STATS

Cluster name: The Beehive
Type of cluster: open
Number of stars: about 1,000
Location: Cancer (see p.95)
Visible: along the ecliptic (Northern and Southern Hemispheres)
Best seen: March to April

HOW TO SPOT

Both the Beehive Cluster and its constellation home of Cancer (see p.95) are quite faint. To locate it, start by finding Regulus in Leo (see p.96). Then find Castor and Pollux in Gemini (see p.95). Look halfway between these points and you should see the Beehive twinkling gently.

STAR STORY

In ancient times, the Greeks and Romans referred to this cluster as Praesepe, meaning 'manger'. They saw two of the stars in the constellation Cancer as donkeys eating from a manger of stars. Chinese astronomers saw the cluster as ghosts in a carriage. Today, it is more commonly known as the Beehive.

THE PLEIADES

Shining brightly in the night sky, the Pleiades is one of the best-known star clusters. With just the unaided eye, you should be able to see several stars shining separately. Use your binoculars or a telescope, and even more stars will appear!

THE STATS

Cluster name: The Pleiades
Type of cluster: open
Number of stars: more than 1,000
Location: Taurus (see p.94)
Visible: along the ecliptic (Northern and Southern Hemispheres)
Best seen: November to February

STAR STORY

With seven of its stars fairly easy to spot, this star cluster is named after seven sisters in Greek mythology (see p.77), although in fact the seventh star dims in brightness and might be harder to see.

YOUNG STARS

The Pleiades is an open cluster of very hot stars. These stars shine with a striking blue tinge. They are young in star terms – only around 100 million years old, which means they've been around for less time than some dinosaurs!

JEWEL BOX CLUSTER

This celestial gem was named by English astronomer John Herschel, who described it as a superb piece of jewellery with precious stones: the jewel box of the sky!

NIGHT JEWELS

The stars in the Jewel Box are likely only 7-6 million years old, making this one of the youngest clusters. They shine blue and red, like sapphire and ruby gems.

THE STATS

Cluster name: Jewel Box Cluster
Type of cluster: open
Number of stars: just over 100
Location: Crux (see p.65)
Visible: Southern Hemisphere and southern parts of the Northern Hemisphere
Best seen: March to September

HOW TO SPOT

This sparkling cluster is located near the bright stars of the constellation Crux (see p.65). Look for a fuzzy patch with the unaided eye. With your binoculars or a telescope, look for the brightest stars forming a pyramid shape.

OMEGA CENTAURI

This mega cluster might be the biggest star cluster in the Milky Way. Its 10 million stars are packed tightly together.

CHANGING STORY

Ancient Greek astronomer Ptolemy thought this cluster was a single star. It wasn't until telescopes were invented that astronomers could see there was more to it. First, they thought it was a nebula. Then, in the 1830s, English astronomer John Herschel recognised it as a star cluster.

THE STATS

Cluster name: Omega Centauri
Type of cluster: globular
Number of stars: about 10 million
Location: Centaurus (see p.85)
Visible: Southern Hemisphere and southern parts of the Northern Hemisphere
Best seen: April to May

HOW TO SPOT

Omega Centauri is best seen from the Southern Hemisphere (see p.116), but it is sometimes visible from southern parts of the Northern Hemisphere. On a clear evening in April or May, locate Spica in Virgo (see p.96) then look towards the horizon to find Omega Centauri – it looks like a fuzzy, faint star.

Omega Centauri is the brightest globular cluster that we can see from Earth.

NEBULAS

Nebulas are clouds of gas and dust in space. There are many different types, providing lots of beautiful sights for stargazers like you to find.

Crab Nebula, as photographed by NASA's Hubble Space Telescope (see p.111)

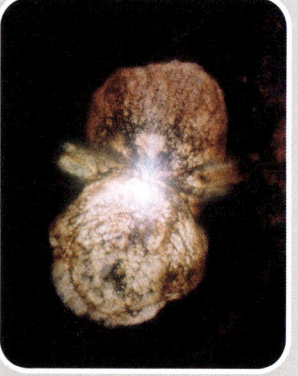

Supernova explosion

STELLAR CYCLE

Many nebulas form in supernova explosions, when red supergiant stars burn out (see p.61). The stellar matter bursts out into space, and some of it collects into a nebula cloud. These nebulas become star factories, where brand-new stars are born. Other nebulas are formed by gas and dust already in interstellar space.

STELLAR TIP

To truly appreciate the beauty of a nebula, try to gain access to a large telescope. But don't worry if you can't – some nebulas can be seen with the unaided eye too! Turn to pages 110–111 for guidance.

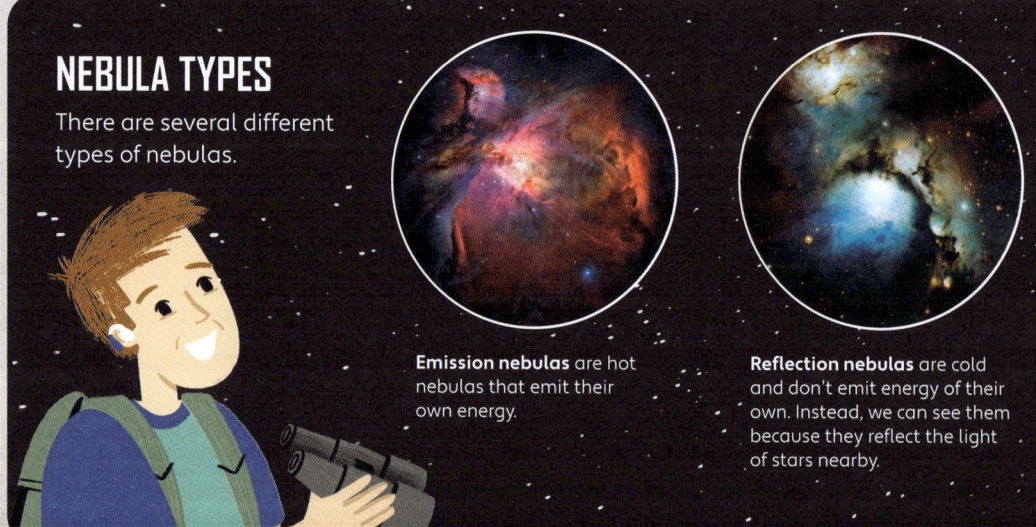

NEBULA TYPES

There are several different types of nebulas.

Emission nebulas are hot nebulas that emit their own energy.

Reflection nebulas are cold and don't emit energy of their own. Instead, we can see them because they reflect the light of stars nearby.

NEBULA NAMES

Although nebulas have official names made up of letters and numbers, many stargazers prefer to use their common names. These often describe the shape of the nebula and tend to be much more fun, such as the Turtle Nebula, the Dandelion Puffball, the Stingray Nebula, the Spare Tyre Nebula and even the Lemon Slice Nebula!

The Stingray Nebula (above) is the youngest planetary nebula known.

Infrared telescope at the European Southern Observatory (ESO), Chile

DIFFERENT VIEWPOINTS

Scientists use different types of telescopes (see p.25) to view nebulas. In addition to traditional telescopes that see light, they use infrared telescopes to view energy coming from stars blocked by dust. Radio and X-ray telescopes can also gather other types of information to give scientists a fuller picture.

Dark nebulas block out the light of the stars behind them, so from Earth we see them as dark patches in the sky. Space telescopes can capture a much clearer picture (above).

Planetary nebulas occur when average stars (see pages 60–61) die. They usually have a clearer shape than other nebulas, often appearing bright and round – like a planet!

Supernova remnants are clouds of gas and dust left behind after a massive star explodes.

ORION NEBULA

Within the mighty constellation of Orion (see p.77) lies this special star-forming nebula, which is just about visible to the unaided eye.

THE STATS

Name: Orion Nebula or M42
Type of nebula: emission
Location: Orion (see p.77)
Visible: Northern Hemisphere and most of the Southern Hemisphere
Best seen: January to February

HOW TO SPOT

First locate Orion's belt (see p.77). Then look to the line of stars hanging down, forming the hunter's sword. Halfway along the sword is a fuzzy patch – this is the Orion Nebula!

While the Orion Nebula appears as a faint, fuzzy area to the unaided eye, a good telescope will show it in much more detail.

THE TRAPEZIUM

Four bright stars within the Orion Nebula form a shape known as the Trapezium.

RING NEBULA

As you might guess, this nebula appears to look like a round ring. Through a small telescope, stargazers love to search for its fuzzy white shape.

BRIGHTER ON THE OUTSIDE

A planetary type, the Ring Nebula was formed from a dying average star. The star itself, now a white dwarf (see p.61), shines so dimly at the centre that it is hard for us to see. However, the material thrown off into space glows brightly around the central star in a sphere. We see this as a ring from Earth.

STELLAR FACT

This nebula is expanding every second and will continue to do so for at least 10,000 more years.

THE STATS

Name: Ring Nebula or M57
Type of nebula: planetary
Location: Lyra (see p.70)
Visible: Northern Hemisphere and part of the Southern Hemisphere
Best seen: July to August

HOW TO SPOT

Locate the stars Sulafat and Sheliak in Lyra (see p.70) and draw a line between them. The Ring Nebula sits just over halfway along this line.

CARINA NEBULA

Four times the size of the Orion Nebula, the vast Carina Nebula contains several areas where new stars are formed.

ETA CARINAE

Near the centre of this nebula is Eta Carinae, a massive star in the later stages of its life. This star dims and brightens over time. Eventually, it will explode in a supernova.

STELLAR FACT
Eta Carinae is more than 100 times more massive than the Sun.

THE STATS
Name: Carina Nebula
Type of nebula: emission
Location: Carina (see p.87)
Visible: Southern Hemisphere
Best seen: March

STARGAZER CHALLENGE
On a clear night, you might be able to spot the Carina Nebula with the unaided eye. Locate it in the Carina constellation (see p.33 and p.87).

CRAB NEBULA

With binoculars or a small telescope, look in the constellation Taurus (see p.94) for this bright supernova remnant – the remains of a star that exploded nearly 1,000 years ago.

PULSING HEART

At the core of this nebula, a pulsar (dense neutron star) spins rapidly, sending out beams of energy that appear to pulse like a lighthouse.

NASA's Hubble Space Telescope has captured incredible photos of this nebula.

THE STATS
Name: Crab Nebula or M1
Type of nebula: supernova remnant
Location: Taurus (see p.94)
Visible: along the ecliptic (Northern and Southern Hemispheres)
Best seen: January to February

NORTHERN & SOUTHERN HEMISPHERES

111

GALAXIES

A galaxy is a system of millions – or even billions – of stars, along with gas and dust. All of this is held together by gravity, and there is often a black hole at the centre.

STELLAR FACT
Scientists believe there are billions of galaxies across the universe.

GALAXY TYPES
There are different types of galaxies, divided by their shape.

Galaxy NGC 474

Elliptical galaxies are round or oval-shaped, like a rugby ball.

Galaxy M74

Spiral galaxies look like large pinwheels in the sky. Spiral arms swirl out from a central bulge surrounded by a disc. These are the most common galaxy types and include the Milky Way.

Galaxy NGC 3489

Lenticular galaxies have a bulge at the centre and a surrounding disc, but no spiral arms.

Galaxy UGC 12682

Irregular galaxies have unusual – or irregular – shapes that aren't as clear as the other types.

HOME GALAXY

Our home galaxy is the Milky Way. Earth, the Sun and the rest of the objects in our Solar System are found in one of the arms of this spiral galaxy. Billions more stars make up the spiral, and these are the ones that you'll see in the night sky.

We are here.

When you see a milky band across the sky, you are actually viewing an arm of our spiral galaxy.

ANDROMEDA GALAXY

The Andromeda Galaxy is the nearest spiral galaxy to the Milky Way – and it is twice its size!

LARGER NEIGHBOUR

Our neighbouring galaxy contains about one trillion stars. It is so big and bright that it is one of the most distant things we can see with the unaided eye. It will look like a smudge, a little larger than a full moon. Use binoculars for an even clearer view.

THE STATS

Name: Andromeda Galaxy or M31
Type of galaxy: spiral
Location: Andromeda (see p.76)
Visible: Northern Hemisphere and part of the Southern Hemisphere
Best seen: August to February (Northern Hemisphere) and October to December (Southern Hemisphere)

HOW TO SPOT

When the sky is very dark, look for the 'W' or 'M' shape of Cassiopeia (see p.79). Identify the star Schedar and follow its arrow, which points you towards the Andromeda Galaxy. For another route to the Andromeda Galaxy, turn to p.117.

STELLAR TIP
Try looking just next to where you expect the galaxy to be, and you might find it appears in the corner of your eye.

Andromeda is the only major galaxy you can see with the unaided eye.

NORTHERN & SOUTHERN HEMISPHERES

SMALL MAGELLANIC CLOUD

This galaxy houses up to 3 billion stars. It is what's known as a dwarf galaxy, orbiting the Milky Way.

DUSTY PATCH

Although it is small, the proximity of this galaxy to Earth means we have an excellent view of it. With the unaided eye in the Southern Hemisphere, you can see a dusty patch covering an area of sky as big as ten full moons.

Small Magellanic Cloud

THE STATS

Name: Small Magellanic Cloud
Type of galaxy: irregular
Location: between Tucana (p.84) and Hydrus (p.83)
Visible: Southern Hemisphere
Best seen: all year round

STARGAZER CHALLENGE

Use a telescope to look at the Small Magellanic Cloud. Can you make out any individual stars?

LARGE MAGELLANIC CLOUD

Sitting close to the South Celestial Pole, the Large Magellanic Cloud can be seen with the unaided eye all year long in the Southern Hemisphere.

Large Magellanic Cloud

THE STATS

Name: Large Magellanic Cloud
Type of galaxy: irregular
Location: across the constellations Mensa and Dorado
Visible: Southern Hemisphere
Best seen: all year round

DWARF GALAXY

Just like the Small Magellanic Cloud, this galaxy also belongs to a group of galaxies called dwarf galaxies. With roughly 30 billion stars, it is a small galaxy affected by the Milky Way's gravity. It is one of the closest galaxies to us.

TARANTULA NEBULA

Within the Large Magellanic Cloud is a glowing star nursery called the Tarantula Nebula, where new stars are born.

HOW TO SPOT

Draw a line from Sirius in Canis Major (see p.78) to Canopus in Carina (see p.87). Pass to the right of Canopus and you'll end up at a dusty patch in a dark area of sky – this is the Large Magellanic Cloud.

SOUTHERN HEMISPHERE

ACTIVITY: STAR JOURNEY

Use the stars as stepping stones through the sky. Try these star hopper challenges to locate some incredible celestial sights visible to the unaided eye.

SOUTHERN HEMISPHERE

CHALLENGE: LOCATE OMEGA CENTAURI

Best time to see: December to February

Take a trip through the night sky to find this big and bright star cluster (see p.107).

1. Locate the bright southern constellation Crux (see p.65).
2. Draw an imaginary line from Acrux at the bottom of Crux towards Mimosa.
3. Follow this line into the constellation Centaurus (see p.85), and keep going until you reach Omega Centauri. You'll find it located on top of the centaur's back.

STELLAR TIP

Once you've pinpointed the location, use your binoculars to get a better view.

NORTHERN HEMISPHERE

CHALLENGE 1: LOCATE SIRIUS

Best time to see: January to February

Follow the stars in Orion's Belt to locate Sirius, part of the constellation Canis Major.

1. Look for the constellation of Orion (see p.77).
2. Find Orion's Belt and follow the line of the belt in the direction away from Orion's shield.
3. Continue this line until you reach Sirius, the brightest star in the night sky.
4. From Sirius, see if you can also spot the Winter Triangle (see p.63).

CHALLENGE 2: TAKE A DIFFERENT ROUTE TO THE ANDROMEDA GALAXY

Best time to see: August to March

You already know that you can use the arrow in Cassiopeia to point you to this galaxy (see p.114). Now try this alternative route.

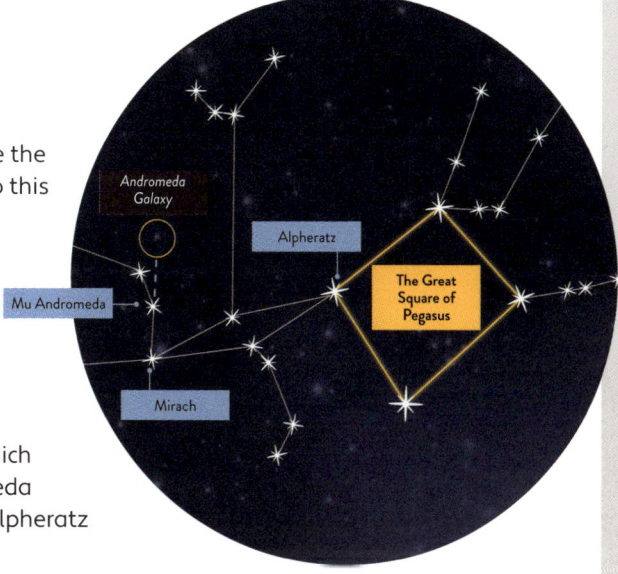

1. Locate the Great Square of Pegasus (see p.74).
2. Find the star Alpheratz in the Great Square.
3. Follow the diamond shape which makes up part of the Andromeda constellation (see p.76) from Alpheratz to the star Mirach.
4. Locate Mu Andromeda, next to Mirach.
5. Draw an imaginary line from Mirach, straight through Mu Andromeda. Follow this line to the Andromeda Galaxy, which looks like a fuzzy smudge.

YOUR STARGAZING DIARY

In your notebook, keep a diary of the sights you see. Use a ruler to draw a grid similar to the one below. Jot down where and when you spotted the object in the night sky. This way you can try to locate it again when the time is right!

OBJECT	TYPE	DESCRIPTION	YOUR LOCATION	DATE	TIME
Jupiter	Planet	Bright object, brighter than the stars	Home (Northern Hemisphere)	December 28th	7:15 pm
Crab Nebula	Nebula	Fuzzy patch	Home (Northern Hemisphere)	January 22nd	7:05 pm
Ursa Major	Constellation	Large constellation, with seven stars making the Plough asterism	Evergreen Park (Northern Hemisphere)	April 17th	9:35 pm

Use this guide to help you identify the names of objects you spot in the sky. Write their names here.

Identify the type of object you've found. Is it a star, constellation, planet, nebula, star cluster, galaxy... or something else?

Note down where and when you saw the object. Be as accurate and detailed as possible.

When you first spot a constellation or planet in the sky, write down all the details of where and when you found it in a logbook.

STELLAR TIP

Use a red-light torch if you are looking at your notebook in the dark.

EQUIPMENT USED	AREA OF SKY	SKETCH OF NIGHT-SKY OBJECT	ANY OTHER NOTES
Unaided eye	East, near orange star Aldebaran		Clear night. Looked like a very bright star!
Telescope	?		Finally managed to see it through Mum's telescope. In Taurus.
Unaided eye	High in the sky		On holiday in Iceland

Did you use your unaided eyes or did you use binoculars or a telescope? If you used a telescope, you could note the magnification too.

If you know it, write down the object's location in the sky: high or low, east or west.

If possible, add a sketch of your sighting here.

Jot down any other info worth noting and remembering, such as something that can help you to find it, or a special colour or detail about the sight.

119

GLOSSARY

Amateur: Someone who does an activity as a hobby rather than professionally for money.

Asterism: A recognisable pattern or group of stars that is not a constellation.

Asteroid: A small rocky object in space that orbits the Sun.

Astronomer: A person who studies astronomy (space and the universe).

Atmosphere: A layer of gas that surrounds a celestial body such as Earth.

Aurora: Colourful moving bands of light in the sky caused by charged particles from the Sun interacting with gases in Earth's atmosphere.

Averted vision: Looking slightly away from an object that you are trying to spot in order to make it appear more clearly.

Black hole: A region of space that has a gravitational pull so strong that nothing can escape, even light.

Celestial: In the sky or in space.

Celestial sphere: An imaginary sphere that surrounds Earth, where we can plot the positions of celestial objects.

Comet: A large object made of ice and dust that orbits the Sun.

Constellation: One of 88 official groups of stars that form a pattern in the sky.

Cosmic: Relating to outer space.

Dark adaptation: The process of your eyes adjusting to low light.

Eclipse: When one celestial body blocks another one from view.

Ecliptic: A line on the celestial sphere that shows the Sun's path through the sky over a year.

Equator: An imaginary horizontal line around the centre of Earth, dividing the planet into Northern and Southern Hemispheres.

Exoplanet: A planet that is outside of our Solar System.

Galaxy: A huge system of gas, dust, millions or billions of stars and their planets, held together by gravity.

Globular cluster: A large group of stars bound closely together by gravity.

Gravity: The force of a planet or other object drawing everything towards its centre.

Hemisphere: One half of Earth.

Horizon: The line where the Sun and sky seem to meet at Earth's surface.

Light pollution: The presence of artificial (human-made) light, which affects the natural light of an area.

Meteor shower: When many shooting stars appear to come from the same area of the sky around the same time.

Nebula: A large cloud of gas and dust in space.

Open cluster: A relatively small group of stars loosely bound together.

Orbit: To continuously move in a circle around a star or a planet.

Planet: A celestial body that orbits a star, has a gravity strong enough to shape it into a sphere and is big enough that its gravity clears the area of objects of similar size.

Planisphere: A map that can be moved to show the stars and constellations visible for a set date and time.

Radio waves: Waves of electromagnetic radiation that can be used for communication across long distances.

Satellite: An object (human-made or natural) that orbits a larger object.

Shooting star: A meteor that moves quickly across the sky and burns up in Earth's atmosphere.

Unaided eye: Using your eyes without any assistance from equipment such as binoculars or telescopes.

Variable star: A star that appears to change in brightness over time.

INDEX

A
Achernar 90
Albireo 71
Aldebaran 32, 80, 94
Alderamin 81
Algedi 98
Algenib 86
Algol 75
Alkalurops 67
Alpha Centauri 33, 85
Alphard 82
Alpha Tucanae 84
Alpheratz 76, 86
Alrisha 99
Altair 72
Andromeda Galaxy 76, 114
Antares 97
Aquarius 99
Aquila 72
Arcturus 67
Aries 94
asterisms 63
asteroid belt 52
asteroids 52
astrology 92-93
Auriga 80
auroras 45

B
Beehive 95, 106
Beta Centauri 33
Beta Hydri 83
Betelgeuse 77
Big Dipper (Plough) 63, 64
binoculars 10, 24
black holes 98
Boötes 67

C
Cancer 95
Canis Major 78
Canis Minor 78
Canopus 87
Capella 80
Capricorn (Capricornus) 98
Capricornus (Capricorn) 98
Carina 87
Carina Nebula 33, 111

Cassiopeia 79
Castor 95
celestial poles 26
celestial sphere 26
Centaurus 85
Cepheid variables 81
Cepheus 81
Cetus 86
Circlet 99
clusters 104-107
Coalsack Nebula 65
comets 53, 54
constellations 59, 62-101
    maps of 28-29, 62
    See also specific constellations
Corona Australis 69
Corona Borealis 68
Crab Nebula 84, 108, 111
Crux (Southern Cross) 64
Cygnus 71

D
Delphinus 86
Delta Cephei 81
Delta Cygni 71
Deneb 71
Deneb Kaitos 86
Dolphinus 86
Double Cluster 105
Draco 66
dwarf galaxies 115
dwarf planets 51

E
Earth 26-27, 44
    eclipses of 40-41
    hemispheres of 26
    layers of 44
    seasons of 27
eclipses 40-41
ecliptic 29
equipment 10-11, 18-19, 24-25
Eridanus 90
Eridanus Supervoid 90
Eta Carinae 33, 87, 111
exoplanets 83

F
Formalhaut 91

G
galactic halo 104

galaxies 112-115
    types of 112
    See also specific galaxies
Galilei, Galileo 18
Gamma Cassiopeia 79
Gamma Velorum (Regor) 88
Gemini 95
Gienah 71
globular clusters 104
Goldilocks Zone 44
Great Hercules Cluster (Messier 13) 104
Great Square of Pegasus 74
Gum Nebula 88

H
Halley, Edmund 54
Halley's Comet 54
Heavenly Waters (Sea of the Heavens) 86
Hercules 73
Herschel
    John 107
    William 18
history of stargazing 15-17
Hubble Space Telescope 19, 53
Hyades 94
Hydra 62, 82
Hydrus 83

I
identification 57
International Space Station 56

J
James Webb Space Telescope 19
Jewel Box Cluster 65, 107
Jupiter 47

K
Keystone 73
Kuiper belt 53
Kuiper, Gerard 53

L
Large Magellanic Cloud 115
Leo 96
Libra 97
light pollution 30
Lippershey, Hans 18
logbook 118-119
lunar eclipses 40-41
Lyra 70

M

mapping the stars 28–29
Mars 46
Mauna Kea Observatory 19
Mercury 42
Messier 13 (Great Hercules Cluster) 104
Messier 81 64
Messier 83 82
Messier 93 89
Messier catalog 21
Messier, Charles 21
meteorites 55
meteoroids 55
meteors 55
meteor showers 55, 67, 75
Milky Way Galaxy 104, 113
Mira 86
Moon 38–39
    eclipses of 40–41
    phases of 28–29
    sides of 38
Mu Cephei 81

N

navigation 17
nebulas 60, 61, 69, 108–111
    naming of 109
    types of 108–109
    See also specific nebulas
Neptune 50
Newton, Isaac 18
North Celestial Pole 26
Northern Cross 71
North Star (Polaris, Pole Star) 32, 81

O

Omega Centauri 85, 107
Oort Cloud 53
open clusters 105
Orion 77
Orion Nebula 77, 110

P

Pancius, Petrus 83, 84
Parsons, William 19
Pegasus 74
Perseids 75
Perseus 75
Pinwheel Galaxy, Southern (Messier 83) 82
Pisces 99
Piscis Austrinus 86, 91
Pismis 24 75
planets 42–51, 53
    dwarf 51, 53
    gas giant 47–48
    ice giant 49–50
    rocky 42, 43, 44, 46
    See also specific planets
planispheres 29
Pleiades 94, 105, 106
    Southern 33, 87
Plough (Big Dipper) 63, 64
Pluto 51
Polaris (North Star, Pole Star) 32, 81
Pole Star (North Star, Polaris) 32, 81
Pollux 80, 95
Procyon 78, 80
Proxima Centauri 85
Ptolemy 69, 107
Puppis 89

Q

Quadrantids meteor shower 67

R

R Corona Borealis 68
Regor (Gamma Velorum) 88
Regulus 96
Rigel 77, 80
Ring Nebula 70, 110

S

Sadr 71
safety tips for stargazing 31
Sagittarius 98
Sagittarius A* 98
satellites 56
Saturn 48
Schedar 79
Scorpio (Scorpius) 97
Scorpius (Scorpio) 97
Sea of the Heavens (Heavenly Waters) 86
Sickle 96
Sirius 70, 80
Small Magellanic Cloud 84, 115
solar eclipses 40–41
South Celestial Pole 26, 33
Southern Cross (Crux) 64, 65
Southern Pinwheel Galaxy 82
Southern Pleiades 33, 87
Spica 96
star clusters 104–107
stars 60–61
    clusters of 104–107
    life cycle of 60–61
    maps of 28–29
    measuring distance between 27
    See also Sun
Stingray Nebula 109
Stonehenge 17
Summer Triangle 72
Sun 36–37
    eclipses of 40–41
supernovas 61, 108
Swift-Tuttle comet 75

T

Tarantula Nebula 115
Taurus 94
T Corona Borealis 68
Teapot 98
telescopes 10, 18–19, 25, 109
tips for stargazing 12–13, 30–31, 57
Trapezium 110
Tucana 84

U

Uranus 49
Ursa Major 63, 64
Ursa Minor 64

V

Vega 70
Vela 88
Vela Pulsar 88
Venus 43
Vesta 52
Virgo 96

W

Winter Hexagon 80
Winter Triangle 63, 78

Z

Zeta Puppis 89
Zubeneschamali 97

CREDITS

The publisher would like to thank the following for their kind permission to reproduce their images:

Key: t = top; b = bottom; c = centre; r = right; l = left; bg = background

Alamy: p.18-19 Science History Images (l), The Granger Collection (t); p.28-29 fototext BCN (tr), Nature Picture Library (r)

Getty Images: p.16-17 duncan1890 (r); p.18-19 ZU_09 (bl)

Shutterstock: Cover – Artsiom P, 19 STUDIO, yoojiwhan, Pavel Chagochkin, berrydog, Ljupco Smokovski, Irina Usmanova, Elena11, carlinjack1, Nerthuz

All pages – tofutyklein (bg), mikesj11 (bg); p.3 icemanphotos; p.4-5 Souliya choummanivong (bg); p.8-9 G.roman (ct), sNike (tr); p.12-13 Rick Whitacre (l), Monkey Business Images (r); p.14-15 rawpixel.com; p.16-17 Stig Alenas (l); p.18-19 momomi (bg), Here (bg), Dima Zel (br), Eduard Moldoveanu (tr); p.20-21 Delpixel (tr) NASA images (r); p.22-23 Chonlatee42 (bl), Makarov Konstantin (bl), AstroStar (tl), Sergey Ryzhov (tr); p.26-27 stockshoppe (br); p.28-29 oxameel (c), Souliya choummanivong (bg); p.30-31 EpicStockMedia (tl), KIDSADA PHOTO (r), AstroStar (tr); p.32-33 foxyliam (tl, bl and tr), Brian Donovan (cr); p.34-35 Vadim Sadovski; p.36-37 Freedom365day (cr), Eugene_Photo (br); p.38-39 Delpixel (l and r), Ahsious_786 (bc), Strory (t), Savvapanf Photo (tr); p.40-41 Fabian Montano Hernandez (t), aeonWAVE (cl); p.42-43 EGA NANDA (c); p.44-45 Denis Belitsky (br), dioeye (c), Souliya choummanivong (bg); p.46-47 Mouhamed amin (b); p.48-49 NASA images (l); p.50-51 24K-Production (l), Artsiom P (tr); p.52-53 Souliya choummanivong (bg); p.54-55 Craig Taylor Photography(br); p.56-57 Utthapon wiratepsupon (tl), Jacques Dayan (l), InnovativeBase Artistry (cb), Artsiom P (b), Alexx_new (r); p.58-59 Andrey Prokhorov; p.60-61 PK Designs (l and r), Zodar (bg); p.62-63 Pavel Malitskyi (tl), Allexxandar (bl), Zodar (bg); p.64-65 foxyliam (l and r), Giovanni Benintende (cl), Brian Donovan (c and cb), Creative Photo Corner (br); p.66-67 foxyliam (l and r), Albert Barr (bl); p.68-69 foxyliam (l and r), Nazarii_Neshcherenskyi (bl); p.70-71 foxyliam (l and r); p.72-73 foxyliam (l and r); p.74-75 foxyliam (l and r); p.76-77 foxyliam (l and r), Lukas Trixl (l), Robert James Behan (b), Erkki Makkonen (br); p.78-79 foxyliam (l and r), Pike-28 (br); p.80-81 foxyliam (l and r); p.82-83 foxyliam (l and r), Wolfgang Kloehr (b), Pike-28 (cb); p.84-85 foxyliam (l and r), Tragoolchitr Jittasaiyapan (cl); p.86-87 foxyliam (l and r); p.88-89 foxyliam (l and r); p.90-91 foxyliam (l and r); p.92-93 GoodStudio (tl), Salomi art (cl), Shyntartanya (bl), Olga Padenko (r), foxyliam (br), NASA images (bg); p.94-95 foxyliam (l and r); p.96-97 foxyliam (l and r); p.98-99 foxyliam (l and r); p.104-105 Martin Dugas73 (l); p.106-107 Serrgey75 (bl), Brian Donovan (cr), Ezequiel Etcheverry (br); p.108-109 Douglas James Butner (cbl), underworld (b), NASA images (bl and br), Amp (cr); p.110-111 Robert James Behan (tl), Outer Space (tr), NASA images (br); p.114-115 foxyliam (b), Antares_StarExplorer (l), AURORA Tomasz Zywczak (br); p.116-117 foxyliam (l and r); p.126-127 icemanphotos

Others: Cover – ESO, NASA/JPL-Caltech/University of Arizona, NASA, NASA/JPL, USAF

p.20-21 NASA, ESA, S. Beckwith (STScI), and the Hubble Heritage Team (STScI/AURA) (cr); p.32-33 NOIRLab:NSF:AURA (tr); p.36-37 NOAA

(c), NASA (br); p.40-41 NASA (bl); p.42-42 NASA/Johns Hopkins University Applied Physics Laboratory/Carnegie Institution of Washington (l), NASA/JPL-Caltech (r); p.44-45 NASA (bl); p.46-47 NASA/JPL-Caltech (l), NASA (tr); p.48-49 NASA/JPL-Caltech (r), NASA/JPL/STScI (br); p.50-51 NASA/Johns Hopkins University Applied Physics Laboratory/Southwest Research Institute (r and br); p54-55 Stuart Atkinson (tl and tr), Halley Multicolor Camera Team, Giotto Project, ESA (bl); p.70-71 NASA (bl); p.74-75 NASA (cr); p.84-85 ESA:Gaia:DPAC (cl); p.88-89 ESO (bl), Sergio Eguivar (tr); p.90-91 ESO (bl); p.94-95 Davide De Martin & the ESA:ESO:NASA Photoshop FITS Liberator (cl), Space Telescope Science Institute Office of Public Outreach (bl), NASA (br); p.98-99 EHT Collaboration (tl); p.102-103 NASA, ESA, and the Hubble Heritage Team (STScI/AURA); p104-105 Davide De Martin & the ESA/ESO/NASA Photoshop FITS Liberator (tr), NASA Mårten Frosth (br); p106-107 NASA Stuart Heggie (tl); p108-109 NASA, ESA, NRAO/AUI/NSF, and G. Dubner (University of Buenos Aires) Space Telescope Science Institute Office of Public Outreach (tl), NASA (l), NASA (tr), ESO (cbr), NASA/JPL-Caltech (br); p.110-111 Thedarksideobservatory (bl); p.112-113 ESA/Hubble & NASA (tl and cbl), ESO/PESSTO/S. Smartt (ctl), NASA (bl), NASA/JPL-Caltech (r); p114-115 J. C. Muñoz/ESO (cr), ESA/Gaia/DPAC,CC BY-SA 3.0 IGO (tr)

ACKNOWLEDGEMENTS

Project managed by Duck Egg Blue Limited

Author: Annie Williamson
Illustrator: Liz Kay
Editor: Kate Baker
Consultant: Stuart Atkinson
Designers: Craig and Kait Eaton
Publishing Director: Piers Pickard
Publisher: Rebecca Hunt
Editorial Director: Joe Fullman
Art Director: Andy Mansfield
Print Production: Nigel Longuet

Published in April 2026 by Lonely Planet Global Ltd

CRN: 554153
ISBN: 9781837586264
www.lonelyplanet.com/kids
© Lonely Planet 2026

Printed in Malaysia
10 9 8 7 6 5 4 3 2 1

All rights reserved. No part of this publication may be reproduced, stored in a retrieval system or transmitted in any form by any means, electronic, mechanical, photocopying, recording or otherwise except brief extracts for the purpose of review, without the written permission of the publisher. Lonely Planet and the Lonely Planet logo are trademarks of Lonely Planet and are registered in the US Patent and Trademark Office and in other countries.

Although the author and Lonely Planet have taken all reasonable care in preparing this book, we make no warranty about the accuracy or completeness of its content and, to the maximum extent permitted, disclaim all liability from its use.

STAY IN TOUCH
lonelyplanet.com/contact

Lonely Planet Office:
IRELAND
Digital Depot, Roe Lane (off Thomas St), Digital Hub, Dublin 8, D08 TCV4

Paper in this book is certified against the Forest Stewardship Council™ standards. FSC™ promotes environmentally responsible, socially beneficial and economically viable management of the world's forests.